Frances Röena Medini

Edalaino

A Metrical Romance

Frances Röena Medini

Edalaino
A Metrical Romance

ISBN/EAN: 9783744665384

Printed in Europe, USA, Canada, Australia, Japan

Cover: Foto ©Thomas Meinert / pixelio.de

More available books at **www.hansebooks.com**

EDALAINE:

A METRICAL ROMANCE.

BY
F. ROENA MEDINI.

NEW YORK:
COPYRIGHT, 1891, BY
G. W. Dillingham, Publisher,
SUCCESSOR TO G. W. CARLETON & CO.
MDCCCXCII.
[*All Rights Reserved.*]

To Her
whose memory is a heritage above price; an example of a great soul; a noble mind; a meek spirit and proud bearing, this volume is inscribed by a
Daughter
who was nurtured in the sunshine of a mother's unbounded love.

Since she doth sleep,—laurel or rue,
'Tis one to me.

EDALAINE.

BOOK I.

Far in the North, where winter halves the year,
A peaceful summer scene in memory dwells,
Above, a canopy of azure pure;
Beneath, its counterpart—a tapestry
Of living green, whose hues are multiplied
By every passing breeze, and which like seas,
In restless waves receding from their shores,
In soft and rhythmic undulations, rolls
From rocky cliffs, to melt like morning mist
In shadowy outlines of the fringing air.

A prairie broad, where naught but nature's self
The harmonies of sight and silence blends,
Where all is life, and yet no conscious life
Is found, except the crimson-throated bird
That darts on high, and then descends to wheel
With lazy wing above the shuddering grass.
Where gentle zephyrs bear across the plain
The clouds to cast a shade, or chase a ray
Of glittering sun far o'er the changing scene.
Amidst these rolling plains, these prairies vast,
There slept a valley, watched unnumbered years
By jealous eye of day, ere man appeared.
Like beauteous Gyneth in her sleep, the vale
Is robed in lustrous garb, and all the charm
Of nature's wealth is laid upon her breast.
Such garniture of leaf and vine was here,
When first the vale imprisoned sight of man,
The gentle falling slope seemed nest of bird,
Whose frame of bending twigs and clinging grass

Is softly lined with silky leaves of green.
For miles around, North, East, and South and West,
Tall grasses wave like helmits plumed, or bend
To breathe o'er heads of wildwood ferns or flowers,
A symphony of chivalry and love.
And through the vale, like moonlight's trembling ray,
That draws a silken thread o'er sleeping seas,
There windeth, too, a line of gleaming light,
Which breaks into a brooklet's murmuring song,
And lulls the listener's anxious heart to rest.
And from its sheen perchance was born the name
It bears of Silver Creek, unless it be
From glimpse of tiny fish with silvery scales,
That idly float on crystal wave, or leap
To catch the sun and make the glittering drops
From off their sides, flash changeful rainbow tints
Then, sinking back amidst the mossy rocks,

Leave eddying circles where they disappear,
To dart with lightning speed beneath the wave.
At times the stranger lingered as he passed,
To meditate, and felt himself upborne
To sense of higher needs in human hearts,
And wondered as he stood, all loth to leave,
Why beauty such as this so long escaped
The eye of man, world-weary and in search
Of such a home as might give lasting rest.
For peace, that builds her nest afar from noise
Of crowded towns, here brooded, and the spell
She wove in harmony with nature's own,
Had power to make one feel the pulse of God
Here beat in holy nature's rhythmic life.
And Reverence, long dead to worldly men,
Here touched to living springs the human heart.
A rocky glen was hid beneath the hills
That bound the northern side, a place where one
In woven dreams would build the fairies' home.

Th' anemones that scarce could blush to hues
Not borrowed from the snow, until their white
Was mixed with purple that Aurora lent
To them! Were these not fairies peeping forth
From earth, while yet the snow in patches decked
The ground?

  Then when the spring brought perfumed air,
They came as violets like bits of sky
To dot the mossy banks, while overhead
The lichens clinging to the trees, subdued
To quaker garb of silver gray, what else
Had seemed too bright a scene.

      At autumn time,
The fairies flee before the clan that stay
And seize the glen and revel gypsy-wise,—
A yearly week of rout and carnival,
And then the glen to merry shout and jest,
To laughter loud awakes. Prolonged halloos
Start timid beasts from out their lair, to speed

From sounds that bode them ill. But flight pro-
vokes
A gay pursuit across the fields, and through
The glen, of rabbit, squirrel or deer, full sure
If lost, another day will bring them down
To click of steel as pitiless as sure.
Rough men and browner women they, whose cares
Ne'er led them ask what copse would shelter them
At night, and none e'er knew from whence they
came,
Or whither went these merry wanderers.
One year, when miracles revealed themselves
In tiny blades that pierced the sod, to give
A spring-time greeting to the sun, when buds
Burst bonds (like butterflies whose chrysalids
We thought the sign of death), to spread their
wings
And flutter o'er the waking earth, there stood
Beside the stream a son of toil, who brought

The simplest tools of builder's art, to make
The hills from morn till night resound to strokes
That echoed o'er the jagged cliffs, as if
Each echo were a foot-fall of the past,
That fled before the coming of the new.
At first the branching oak and stately pine,
That firm as warriors 'gainst the pelting lead
Of arméd hosts, had warded off the blasts
Of winter storms and stood a hundred years,
He felled, bringing to nature's law the art
Of man. For days he toiled, until, restrained
By rugged walls he raised; the darkling stream
Had paused to mirror on its placid face
The laughing sky, in mimic lake that stayed
Awhile, then leaped its boundaries to be
Again the brooklet of our song, and then
Beneath his iron hand there grew a mill,
And then the stridulous saw, in mocking tones
Sang victory o'er the bleeding grove that long

Had stood a sentinel before the glen.
Perhaps this song that seemed to selfish men
A cheerful lay, lured other sturdy men
To this fair spot, for soon a street was laid,
Rude homes were built, and then, not yet content,
A church with modest spire, behold a town!
Too soon the spoilers learned whence came the wood,
And like a scar that lives, a haunting ghost
Or gloomy sepulchre which marks the spot
Where innocence a victim fell to crime,
Of all the trees the rugged stumps alone,
(Sad tablets of the soil), were left to prove,
Dame nature had, by years of care, endowed
The vale with forest trees, her hardier work,
And then, as if she long designed that man
Should know remorse, she paused. No later growth
Had she brought forth to give to eager man

Such sad employ. And so, full soon, the mill,
Denied of food for hungry maw, like some
Gaunt vulture, chained upon the whit'ning bones
That he had stripped, becomes a skeleton
Through which the tempest whistles dolefully
Then prone to earth it falls to meet decay.
The church itself grew brown; and happier he
Who trod the pulpit's narrow range, than they
Who cramped themselves on benches rudely made,
To hear a message drawn throughout an hour,
By dint of lengthy words and gestures fierce,
That save as task work he had told in half
The time.
      Long years was this before our tale
Begins. The stones beneath the dam were black
With slime, and only snakes on summer days
Betook themselves to this old spot to bask
In sunshine. Coiled in glittering rings they
    blinked

Or slept in lazy comfort, nor took pains
To charm a careless bird that chanced too near.
One day, when disappeared the sun in space
Behind the western hill, and left a glow
Of promise for a new and perfect day,
A band of earnest men and women paused
Upon the summit of the hill, and gazed
With weary, aching limbs, and throbbing brows,
Upon the vale where shrub and leafy tree,
Half hid, and half revealed the spire, the school,
And winding road that passed close by the mill.
A silence fell upon both young and old.
The haven here was found at last, to lay
The corner-stone of faith which they believed
Would falsify all lesser creeds, and bring
The earthly happiness which mortals crave.
A solemn prayer arose from out each heart,
And silently they went adown the hill
To this new life which promised all to them,

Yet to how few it kept its promises!
Time prospered them,—this band that wish'd to prove
The world at fault in only selfish aims,
And gave up all to mutual help and love.
Alas, such trials oft by earnest souls
Have failed, nor can we chide them for their good
Intent,—for they have suffered most to find
That souls there are, too small, too weak to bear
The burden of the unattempted rights,
And only serve to mar the brave attempts
Of nobler souls they fail to comprehend.
They dwelt as brothers should, while strictly bound
Within the rules that marked their new belief,
Or rather old belief, and new endeavor.
They daily gathered round the cheering board,
One common kin, ignoring ties of blood.
And those who came to join their swelling ranks,

Endowed with greater wealth, as freely gave
Into the common store, as if all things
He used before had never been his own.
And thus they prospered, till the name they chose
Of Phalanx spread abroad; and to its fold
Were added thoughtful, noble, learnéd men.
And here events as elsewhere on the earth,
Swift followed each to burn in human hearts,
The memories that serve as mile-stones oft
Upon the rugged road that leads through life.
Forever rushing toward the goal we hope
Is yet remote, we hasten on with speed
That's ever undiminished, hot to meet
We know not what, and yet assured 'tis death.
A day of mirth, a hush that seemed like death,
Brought change or care, made hearts beat gay or sad,
Now touched one lintel, now passed by to pause
And tap upon a worthy neighbor's door.

Three years had passed, and Andrew Grant, who came
With children six to swell, with manly pride,
The chorus of the dreaming Fourierites,
Had builded him a roomy house of stone,
Which mother earth had yielded him with strong
Resistance, yet, I ween, with less of pain
Then when she saw the budding trees cut down,
And felt within her veins the milk she fed
Them with, first over-run and then turn dry.
And why was this? Ask thou the mother heart,
Which claims her painful care, the child that draws
From her his daily life, or him who stands
No longer nurtured by her rich, warm blood!
Good Andrew Grant, unmindful of dumb earth,
Felt much of pride in this his noble work,
And hastened to complete it, there to give
With parent's fond demur, his eldest born,
Elizabeth, in wedlock to John Holme,

The miller's son, the bravest huntsman round.
And blessings manifold were on them shower'd,
While parents sigh'd and said, "'Tis such events
That warn us life indeed is short, our babes
But yesterday, to-day, alas, are gone!"
In winter time the younger folk took joy
In sports wherein the elders saw no ill,
And simple dances marked to time of flute
And viol, filled the happy evening hours.
So winter passed, when came the bans of one
They greatly loved, and here it seemed that not
The mazes of the dance had linked two hearts,
For he whose flute made dreamily the waltz
Go round, would never dance: "My brains," he said,
"Were never meant to guide my awkward feet."
But certainly his eyes had dwelt full oft
Upon a fragile form, that midst the dance
Had woven webs to catch unwary hearts.

And so Dean Brent awoke to lay aside
His flute, and bravely woo the shrinking maid.
'Twas this event that brought to them Dame Ann,
His kindly mother, straight from Edinburgh.
"'Twas hard," she said, "just found, to gie him up."
And none had dreamed, I ween, how deep her grief
Took root, and none perhaps could understand
Her loneliness, unless it be the wife
Of Andrew Grant, Dame Evelyn; whose heart
Was filled with generous love for all mankind,
And touched with sympathies so swift and sure,
She straight could read and feel their griefs e'en when,
For good to them, she gaily laughed and sought
To make them seem scarce worthy of a sigh.
And yet what charm of nature could replace
The chain of habit in the agéd, born

'Mid smoke, and stir, and roll of wheels, and din
Of city life? The bells that toll'd a death;
That chimed the evening call to prayer; the bells
That merrily a marriage rite proclaimed,
Or angrily did beat their iron tongues
Against the sounding brass in wild dismay,
Lest unaware the dwellers of its streets,
Too late, alas, should find themselves wrapped round
By fire,—all these, within the quiet vale
Were never heard. The very Sabbath day
Itself seemed not the same, but changed to peace
Of country life, its beauty was to her
A sealéd book and cause of vague unrest.
But angels, not unmindful of the tired
And lonely soul, caught first a wish that springs
From earnest loving hearts, a ray of sun
To link to cheerfulness a seed of truth;
A kiss of innocence and chastity;
An atom of humanity, and pledged

Them all to keeping of Dame Evelyn,
Who lived in noble practices the dower
Of beauteousness she prayed to give her child.
"She shall be pure and true," she said, and faith
Made fairer yet the mother's countenance,
And virtuous herself, no wrong would come
To chill the blood within her womb. She sought
In all her vision rested on, the fair
And loveliest. Like mirror to reflect
Within its darkling depths, what passes o'er
Its face, so, she believed : "Whate'er my soul
Doth know, doth feel, doth contemplate, shall stay
Reflected on the mind of this my child.
What joy to be the chosen instrument
Of God in leaving impress on our seed!"
She read, and when her thoughts revealed the true,
Or pure, or noble in the word of man,
Philosopher, or poet born, she said :
"So would I that my child interpreted

The good of life." She gazed upon a work
Of art, and lingered long upon its points
Of excellence, to form the younger life
To observation close which can alone
Perfect. A spirit dwelt beside her, which
She taught, and teaching thus she grew herself.
In dreams of good to man and pray'r to God,
Dame Evelyn's steps seemed now no more of
    earth.
All attributes of life, its sympathies,
Its tender helpfulness and mercy shown,
Fair truth, unselfishness and saving word,
All graces, virtues that she wished bestowed,
She lived, and shrank with horror from the faults
That would have marred a perfect life.
                                Where found
She most these practices? Upon the hearth
Of home, whose toil began at break of day,
And ended not till clocks had toll'd their length

Of hours, to turn and count them yet again.
Avarice, envy, malice, all were robbed
Of poisonous intent, by charity;
By love of neighbor as herself and more.
The wholesome practice of the Golden Rule.
"I do to them as I would have my child
Done by." The petty trials that beset
This life, could touch her not. An angry word,
Complaint, or peevishness met such a look
Of gentleness, such ready, calm reply,
It quieted the troubled breast like balm
Upon a burning wound, an angel's touch
Whose wing had chanced to dip too near the earth.
And so it was, a presence sanctified,
Her spirit walked with God, her feet with men.
An angel might have lost his holiness,
Combining thus the ills of life with will
Of God. They might? Nay, we belie belief.
It is not death that gives the angel birth,

'Tis He, that, schooled on earth, has beautified
A nature prone to fault, till God-like, bears
He impress of the noble right to act
For God, throughout the spaces of the high
And glorious kingdom of perfected souls.
Oh, heart of mothers! You alone can know
The rapture born within the soul when filled
With consciousness of power to make or mar
A budding life! Oh, days of hope and trust;
Of fear and pain; of doubt and helplessness;
Inevitable mysteries of birth and death!
Of dreamings in the expectant mother's heart,
Of fancies built on fret-work of desire!
What most she loves is colored in these dreams.
What most desires, in minds of men observes,
And scarcely conscious of the wish, a prayer
Like incense wafts its perfume to the skies,
And thus sustained by nature's yoke she bears
Of shadowed martyrdom, the mother walks

With joy:—" For though I die,"—faith speaks—
    "my child
May live, her sweetness tempering ills of life,
Her truth disarming sin."
                  Though seventh bairn
Of Andrew Grant and Mistress Evelyn,
The love that waited her, intensified
By feeling that she was the last, could note
The touch of angel hands, and so they called
Her Edalaine and prayed "that faith might guide
Her life till angels roll'd the stone from off
The tomb of buried hopes, to give them back
Again." So said Dame Evelyn that night.
At first the eyes that opened to the day,
Seemed violets that glistened through a lake
Of morning dew, and then, as if the sun
Had mixed its red with blue of skies and touched
Once more the orbs that glowed with laughter ere
The lips could form a radiant smile; these depths

That prophesy a soul's expanse were turned
To purple hues.   With passing summer months
The angels touched her eyes again, this time
With hues they borrowed from the brownest leaf
Of autumn, or the chestnut as it falls
To catch the glint of setting sun that warms
Its brown with ruddy gold.

      Sweet eyes! They brought
A benediction in their glance.   But most
Of all the blessings fell in lonely heart
Of good Dame Ann, who called her " Peaceful
  Eyes,"
And straight declared her born to some great work
On earth, to which the mother ready gave
Assent.   "She's born to be the comforter
Of fast approaching wintry days, the sun
And light of seared and yellow age. What life
Its plenitude to richer charity
Bestowed, could mortals find?"   But silently

The other turned to hide a starting tear,
That, midst the furrows of her brownéd face,
Found paths washed deeply in by bitter brine
Of griefs, now wept a score of dreary years.
Then, gazing down upon the sleeping child
With something like a sob that stirred her voice,
She spoke: "I ken its like, guid wife, but then,
You see, I thocht the same o' my wee lad,
And now he's ta'en a braw young wife wha's guid
As gowd, and means, I dinna doot, to be
As kind to me as my ain lass, but then,
Ye ken, I canna feel, though fain I would,
There's muckle need o' me about the house,
When a' is said, and if the morn's fair sun
Looked down on me nae mair, its a' the same
To Wullie there." "Fie, Fie, Dame Ann, thy heart
Hath played thee false, thy spirit's sight is dark,

Surcharged with spleen. How gladly, when my
    child
Hath safely reached the poise of womanhood,
Shall I give o'er my care to one whose love
Will guard and waken her to life she else
Would never know! And think you then, I lose
My child? No, no! A son is won! The heart
So narrow that it loves but one, loves not
So well, and mother heart that lavished love
While yet the sleeping bud had never seen
The light, must love her child but for the need
Of loving, nor asks love's return again.
And thy good son, hast thou not yet his face
To look upon; his voice to hear, his care
To prove devotedness?" And here a shade
Fell o'er the sill to slant from off the porch.
"Well said, good Mistress Evelyn, I ween
My mother lacks thy seeing mind. Methinks

My manhood frets her more than cares she knew
In early years. She mourns her babe for aye,
Nor can she think, in spite of all my words,
That Jeannie there, and I, count her in all
Our hopes of joy, our grief, sole lack of pow'r
To banish from her past its memories
Of loss!". "Ah, lad!" and Dame Ann smiled through tears,
"Ye ken, wae's me! ye're mither's aulder grown,
And aibleens like a bairn, ye've nocht to do
But bear wi a' her thrawart ways, and think
It were not ever thus." "Aye, aye!" replied
The son with fond embrace, "there's few sae braw
To look upon e'en yet, just look at this,"
And off comes Dame Ann's cap to bare her head.
"What blushing maiden in our town is crowned
With silky, waving hair like that? Its brown
Is tinged with burnished gold, that through its veins

Runs safely hid till light of sun reveals
It there. And then these pearls! Bright senti-
    nels
Of Epicurius! one only, gone,
And sacrificed to small a thing as pin
That held a ribbon to my kite. One day
I plead her aid to make it fast, and she—
'Tis not ingratitude that bids me say't—
Was quite as much the child as I, that risk'd
Her lovely teeth to pinch the rebel pin
To place. And how I cried when, with a scream,
She caught the broken ivory in her hand!
And she, ' Hist, hist! my lad, ye mauna greet,
Else father hear, and we mun tell him a'.'
" Ha! ha! we made a bonny pair of kids,
Hey, mother, were ye not a saunsie lass?"
" Tut, tut, ye sport my poor Scotch tongue and
    yet
Ye have ye're father's laughter-loving way

Of flattering one, an' now ye've waked the bairn,
An' mussed my cap, so get ye hence to mow
Ye're hay." "I see, my nose has summit wrong,
A joint awry! 'Twill be this babe, that soon
Will muss ye're caps and play the truant o'er
Your days." And so it fell, indeed the child
Became a tiny despot o'er the life
Of Mistress Ann.
        Yet not exempt from griefs
Were those who dwelt within the charmèd vale,
As years, by their events, made short or long,
Passed on and brought fair gifts of love to some,
To others griefs that time could not assuage.
Death came and went. Sometimes he reaped the
    aged,
Sometimes the fairest flow'r that bloomed, as if
Jealous that earth should be so bright, so glad.
One summer day, when nature seemed to doze
And trees to languish 'neath their weight of fruit,

A golden day, when drowsy hum of bees,
That paused to taste with lazy sips the sweets,
That lurk deep sunk in fragrant cups of blue,
Of white or gold, then paused inert upon
The swinging edge, to seek some other field
Of spoil,—the carol of a girlish voice
Awoke the birds like flash of sun against
The shade.

   Oh, Rose
  Of Summer quest,
  Rests in thee no thorn?
  Oh, bird in thy nest,
  Wert thou haply born?
  Shadows fall from every tree,
  Why not they on you and me
   Courage, heart,
   Do not start,
  At a falling leaf.

Elizabeth, as fair and bright to-day
As on that bridal morn when love endowed
Her life with his, came forth to watch John
 Holme's
Return. The song that kissed her lips to thrill
The air with sweetest melody, to die
Of sadness born of fleeting rapture, yet
To kiss, in other notes, her lips' bright red,
Had ceased, till, silently she stood, and then,
As if the flowers had begged the boon to give
Their lives for ecstacy of one full hour
Upon her breast, she clustered crimson buds
Against a leaf of green, and swiftly here
And there, amidst the purple of her braids,
Had nestled them. Herself a flower abloom
In creamy white, her dark rich beauty more
Resplendent 'midst its falling drapery,
And dreamily, as if her twittering friends,

The birds, had whispered her: "Add other flowers,"
She touched her robes with gleaming buds of rose,
Until Titania ne'er was crowned more fair.
And thus she sang :

>Oh, Rose
>In Autumn air
>Hast thou felt no chill?
>Oh, love so fair,
>Fears thy heart no ill?
>Ne'er was sun without a shade;
>Life of care and joy is made,
>Faint not, heart,
>Bear thy part,
>Through a bitter grief!

When music of her voice had ceased in waves
Of sound that left her lips to ring through space,
To disappear amidst ethereal blue,

Like angel footsteps, or the sigh of man,
A clock chimed forth the hour with weird strokes,
Till with the fifth, a whirr of wheels announced
It was the last! A faint surprise crept o'er
Her face, then faded there. "He's late," she said,
"I wonder why," and then from tree to shrub,
From bird to flower, as bright and restless grown,
As e'er the restless wings of humming bird,
Whose tremulous beat keep time to troubled thoughts,
She glided, while she waited anxiously.
Ten minutes passed, when down the shady road
Her husband's dog came rushing madly through
The dust, his coat of shaggy black all wet
And mixed with weeds that line with slimy lengths
The muddy depths above the mill. His haste
Was not of joy, his eyes with anxious sight
Appeal'd to her, and heedless of her robe

He jumped to lay his paws upon her arm
And gave a piteous cry to call her back
When puzzled and amazed she gazed away
As if her husband's coming must be brief,
And yet this cry smote on her straining ear
A message sharp and bitter, plain because
Unused to aught but joy expressing, speech
Yet unprepared, foreboding swept her down
And like a stricken deer, the huntsman's prey,
She, pale and white, sank 'midst the fragrant
    flowers,
Nor felt, nor knew how bravely then he strove,
By nature's true, unerring instinct taught,
To wake again to life the fluttering pulse
That now refused to beat. At last, assured
His efforts were in vain, he gave a cry
Of grief, and then again drew back to gaze
Upon the pallid face, perhaps to raise
An agonized thought to some unknown

And stronger power, then bounded o'er the field,
Till at the old stone school he paused. The door
Was closed. Two hours before, the green had
 ceased
To echo back the calls, the laughs and shouts
Of merry children's sport. But not deterred
By doubts that human minds might then have felt,
He sprang upon the window ledge, and woke
The stern old master from his dreams by quick
And vig'rous pulls upon his threadbare coat.
The master gazed at first with mute surprise,
And then, he seemed to see a human pain
Within the eyes that looked to him, that chilled
The blood within his agéd heart. He seized
His hat, and followed hastily the steps
Of his dumb guide. They passed the busy town,
And met nor man nor beast upon their way.
Howbeit, at the broken bridge arose
A stooping form that held by hand a bright

And winsome child. How fleet is time! The
    babe,
Sweet Edalaine, was queen o'er all thro' love,
And bore the stature of her five short years
Imperious as a queen, that blends with it
Sweet modesty.
                The master seeing them
A moment paused and cried: "Good eve, Dame
    Ann."
You have not chanced to see our worthy friend,
John Holme?" and raised the while his hat to
    wipe
The beads of crystal from his brow. "Aye, that
I have, guid mon, not ha' an hour aback,
Wi' gun in han', an' after that I heard
The gun resound, an' said until mysel',
The cruel sport the lad's begun. I wo'd
He'd see the fearfu' sin o't." "I fear the worst,"

The master said. "Would you, good Dame, make
    haste
To seek his wife and friends, and send me aid
To look for him?" "Aye, that I wull, guid mon!
A better lad ne'er lived, except it be
My ain guid bairn, my Wullie there." But ere
Her words were done, the master scaled the fence,
And stood upon the only plank that crossed
The wild and roaring waters of the dam.
It yielded to his weight, but did not break,
And pausing not to think of dangerous ways,
Nor of defeat in searching for his friend,
He hastened on, intent alone to save.
His guide already stood upon the shore
And bayed in mournful tones, expression sad
Of his belief. When come, he straightway led
The master to a heap of clothes, and when,
As if to tell more plainly where his friend
And master disappeared, he cried and moaned

Again upon the water's edge, and then
Plunged in and swam beneath the willow bough,
And laid a wounded bird upon the shore,
The worst was told. No human tongue could tell
The mournful news in more explicit way,
And naught remained to do but wait for help,
Or rather hasten to the nearest house
For ropes and drags. So once again he braved
The dangers of the old and rotten plank.
Dame Ann, who hurried toward the town, sent young
And old to join the search, and when she near'd
The gate that opened to the cottage door,
Embowered by climbing rose and columbine,
And stood within the precincts of those grounds,
Made beautiful by toil of him they sought,
She felt a hush that moved her more than all
The anxious doubts that fill her heart before.

The hope that naught was wrong seemed then to
    die
Within her heart. Instead, a dread, a sad
Foreboding rose to take its place. She gave
A smothered cry, as she beheld the form
Half hid in grass, and while the others sought
The husband drowned, Dame Ann, at home, tried
    hard
To wake the heart that beat for him to life
And grief, for such was duty. Such are some
Of life's most strange inexplicable laws.
Why could she not have slipped quite out of life,
Unconscious that it held such cruel blows,
Such bitter griefs? But God had not so willed.
We needs must meet the griefs, to comprehend
That life is repetitions of itself,
In woes that blanch the cheek, and joys that cloy
The over-giddy heart, both set, perchance,
As balances to measure out to us

The proper gauge of moral rectitude.
She lived, and woke with words of grievous fright,
That she had swooned by weakness of her will,
In place of hastening to her husband's aid.
Unmindful of the pleadings of Dame Ann,
The tears of infant Edalaine who held
Her sister's dress, and could not understand
Denial of caressing words, she sped
Adown the road that now lay hid in night,
To meet a sad and silent train that bore
By torchlight what was late his breathing form.
These fitful gleams of light! They seemed to glare
With eyes like demons, midst the gloom of deep,
Dark night, to mock her grief! They seemed to sear
The senses of her dizzy brain, and heap
Her agonies with tortures sharp and keen!
The loss of consciousness, but at the thought

Of accident had come; now death was here,
His labor done, relief came not. Each pang
Of grief was hers to know and feel, "'Twere well,"
Some said, "if hearts like hers could break." But hearts
That break are few, and do not, as these words
Imply, bring peace of death. Less pain there'd be
On earth if this could be, for living deaths
Were spared the human heart. One sad, brief hour!
Her happiness a wreck, and life had changed
For her, from gladsome sun to hellish night!
This jailer, gaunt Despair, all pitiless,
Locked in the tempest of her grief to tear
Itself against the bars of prison'd speech.
The night, the lights, the pallid faces, all
Seem'd strange, and then the hidden *Something* there

Upon the rough-formed bier, heaped horror on
The wan, weird darkness of the summer eve!
Another woman would have thrown herself
Upon the corpse, and waked with cries the night,
As hoping to arouse the dead, but she
Seemed paralyzed in all but sense of grief
And sight. Her eyes two burning balls of fire
That sought upon the faces of this dark
And slowly moving throng, some new-born hope
Glanced fearfully and earnestly around.
And when the silent, dripping form was laid
Upon the cottage floor, she gazed at them,
At it, and clung to friendly hands stretched out
In deep-felt sympathy, as if at sight
Thereof some nameless terror of the *Thing*
Stark stiff in death had clutched her timid heart.
And when at last she doubtingly crept near,
Drew from the face a scarf of silk there thrown,
Stroked back the hair, and gently wiped away

The clinging weeds. Unheard, they moved out-
    side,
And in the room alone she knelt, her dead
Her own. A shivering sigh, a half-suppressed
Dry sob,—no other sound spoke of her grief.
One arm up-raised the senseless head, and close
Her trembling lips sought life and love in his,
Then whispered, "Come, O love, my life is thine!
Nay, mine and that of our unborn, is thine—
Drink all from my poor lips, and it shall give
Thee pulse and living warmth. And once again
She clung to lips that seemed straight drawn in
    dumb
Derision, nor sank curve in curve as was
Their wont, till quickening currents of their hearts
Burst bounds of two-fold life, to sweep from soul
To soul in one swift burning tide; and then
She gazed in sightless orbs, as if this sharp
Repulse had stung her heart to newer grief.

She slowly laid the head upon the floor,
Look'd round for sympathy, then thrilled the air
To swiftly eddying circles with a shriek
That pierced the gloom of night, and sobbed itself
To sudden silence.   Stonily she let
Them lead her from the room of death, to sit
In dumbly stricken grief, to slowly join
And rend apart the tender, supple hands
Of snowy white, nor conscious of the pain
To those who watched, beholding grief like this.
Once came Dame Evelyn, and standing there
Pressed to her heart the head distraught, then passed
Her soft, magnetic hands along the brow,
And o'er the agonized uplifting of the eyes,
Long sought to draw a restful veil.   A sob
Came struggling up to parchéd lips, and then,
Like others, died away in shuddering moans.

Hot tears coursed down her mother's cheeks and
    fell
Upon her own, and mother's aching heart
Plead in the gentle music of her words.
"Oh, weep, my daughter, tears were made for
    grief.
I've seen thee weep through tender pity o'er
A wounded bird, and lesser things than that.
Give way to this imprisoned grief! You'll break
My heart with such still agony!" She pressed
Her mother's hand in silence, but no word
Came from the motion of her pallid lips,
And terror for her child began to rend
The heart of Evelyn, that soon this grief
Would blot the reason of her mind. All through
The night, the dead to silence given o'er,
They spent in ceaseless efforts to undo
The silence of her grief, but naught availed.

    Soft twilight kissed the dawn and birds awoke,

To join their songs with preparations vast
Then taking place throughout the mighty realm
Of nature, for the coming of the day.
These woke the tiny Edalaine, who slept,
Oblivious of the desolation brought
Upon her sister's heart. The watch-dog lay
Beside her bed, and rose with her as if
To save her from the phantom grief that reign'd
An uninvited guest within the house.
The breakfast room was near,
And Edalaine, with gladsome heart tripped in,
To find it vacant still. The sunshine fleck'd
The sanded floor, and crept upon the chair,
With ample arms now vacant evermore;
Slipped down to dance fantastic shapes with shade
Before the open door, and lingered 'neath
The vine-clad porch, to kiss and play at hide
And seek with sporting zephyrs there. Just high
Enough to open wide the closet door,

Blithe Edalaine, her brother's gown of blue
Drew forth, and laid upon the oaken chair,
And next dropped soft-lined slippers on the hearth,
When lo! she found the dog had drawn away
The robe, and hid it out of sight again.
Once more the coat was brought, and smoothly laid
Upon the easy chair, but "Gay" was firm.
The slippers now had been replaced, and then
He turned to capture coat and drag it back
Again. This time he placed himself against
The door on haunches firmly set and strong,
And Edalaine could scarce decide if best
To laugh, or scold, or cry, and neither saw
The pallid face that watched them from the door
Till suddenly Elizabeth, the gates
Of grief at last broke down, fell on the neck
Of this dumb beast who sought to save her pain,
And wept in heartfelt pity once again,

Of pity most forlorn, that felt for self.
"Oh Gay, oh Gay! why could you save him not
For me, you are so wise and strong? so kind
And pitiful!"   He laid his head against
Her tear-stained cheek, and kissed, in dog-like
    fashion,
Hands, and cheek, and brow, while Edalaine,
In frightened wonder stood to see her tears,
And gladly ran to hide on mother's breast
Her fears, as, pale with watches of the night,
She too had stopped to dry her own sad tears,
At sight of this pathetic scene. She led the
Child from out the room, "Fear not, my child,
The sun shines bright upon the grass, we'll walk
And talk of things your years have not as yet
By observation taught. The birds will sing,
Though sister weeps, and each fulfill a law
Divine and right."   And then the mother sought,
In words that lent themselves to childish ears,

To tell of death the part more beautiful.
And last explained the endless sleep that bound
The frame of him who walks among his friends
Gaily and free and blithe but yesterday.
"Be ready ever for the last good-night,
My child, nor ever let a single hour
Of coldness or dissension stand between
Yourself and those you love the best, lest one
Or other drop the while in this deep sleep."
The last sad rite had been performed, but she
Who mourned the most, lay tossing on a bed
Of pain. To consciousness she waked but once,
And gazed upon a tiny waxen head,
Whose life was gone ere died upon her lips
The blessing breathed for it, and then the light
Was spent. Delirium swayed the restless mind,
And friends were torn with anxious doubts lest
    death

Again returned, should conquer life and prove
This soul too frail for battling with such griefs.
Day crowded days to weeks, and weeks to months,
And leaves took on their autumn tints of brown.
Fruit fell to earth, and then the leaves dropped
    down
To bury what man left to turn to dust.
The birds began to leave their nests and hie
Themselves to sun-bathed, leafier climes ere woke
The wife to consciousness of widowhood,
Which seemed to blot the grief of childlessness.
The dog, a faithful guard, watched night and day
Beside the couch, and often Edalaine
Would sit betwixt his paws to watch with him,
And wondered o'er and o'er if this wan face
Was yet in life, or whether sleep—the last
Deep solemn sleep had claimed the suffering one,
And, nestled close beside the shaggy dog,

Her childish heart poured forth its fear and woe
In many a simple, earnest prayer to save
To them her sister's life.

BOOK II.

When, in the story of the world's increase,
Have not the evil passions of its men,
Like subtle, smouldering fires amid the green
And towering giants of the forest glades,
Crept in the nobler virtues to destroy,
Till souls, the blackened shadows of themselves,
Desolate remained? And in what age of man
Hath not each sin found creeds, whose sophistry
Baptized belief or act as virtue's self?
And that men by nature great have oft belied
Their gifts of virtue, whence all wisdom springs,
When inclination warped belief, or wrought
With reasonings as false as fair, to lead

A life of whim and mad caprice undreamed
By purer minds!   Why think our age exempt?
Alas!   Mistakes breed everywhere within
The range of human frailty, like rude weeds.
And so to those who dwelt within the vale,
Though not at once, was brought a wondrous change.
Blind man would say an evil power had wrought
The change in simple envy that a spot
On earth should boast of peace and harmony.
But why not say that God, far-seeing, wise,
Knows best, and that a peaceful life on earth
Would deaden new resolve and fresh endeavor.
But whether came the change by will of God
Or friend, a serpent crept into the vale,
O'er many thresholds passed to leave behind,
Its slimy trail.   Fair homes were broken up,
And inmates scattered far and wide, while men
Became the victims of its deadly charm,

And minds in struggling 'twixt conflicting right
And wrong, and mysteries which confounded
 them,
Or filled with phantasies absurd, were crazed,
Were left like vessels tossed at sea, no sun,
No compass, guide or anchor, midst the storm
That drove them wide. And yet the cause of this,
They call by sacred name of Love. I wot
That there are those will shudder as they read,
And understand what shame, what grief was
 brought
Into the vale by sophistries whose name
E'en now my pen abhors to write.
And much as in the days of yore temptation came
To pliant man, in woman's gentle form,
But here the likeness ends. This later Eve
Had envied man his rights, and, wond'ring why
He seemed to claim what was denied to her
(The chief of these the right to live in sin),

She mused, compared, and caught the secret
 thought.
'Twas dress that made a woman slave. A man
Was free to stride, to joy in actions. Coils
Of silky tresses weighted not his brain ;
The ancient story told of Samson's strength
Was but a myth, and, earnest in demand
Of rights usurped by man, she never joy'd
O'er secrets that enfold man's heart when drawn
By woman with a single golden hair.
This daily toil of braiding tresses, too,
Was quite enough to give the men a start
By one full hour, and that, in one short year,
Would make a month of working time,
In life of every woman born (for oft
The silly ones were known to dress the hair
Full twice each day), was nearly fifteen years
Within allotted life of man! Ah! yes,
'Twas plain, the hair must go, and then, since time

Had much increased the vanity of dress,
So great their waste of hours it ne'er could be
In decimals compared, and now that minds
Had lost the simple taste of Adam's Eve,
And dress, they must, at least no vantage ground
Should more be left to man, and so the dress
Must change. To imitate the man? Oh, no!
The dress was hers as much as his, by all
Good rights, and soon they'd see how smooth the
    wheels
Of State would move in woman's hands. With this
Resolve, she sought to cover o'er the curves
Of lines that marked her beauty over man's,
Until she half forgot her sex, and thought
Herself creation's Lord! Not now content
With face to win, with grace to charm, with voice
To allure, she 'gan to strive to couple with
Her limbs of fawn-like grace man's vigor, then
To tune the lute strings of her woman's voice

To clarion notes, and rather wake the world
To raging war in crying down its wrongs,
Than first to tame its passions' flame to use
More sweet, by sounds that lured to harmony
The jangling discords of its outraged souls.
And one of these had wandered to the vale.
The name they bore of fearless enterprise
In living out their code, seemed fitting place
To plant the seed that soon would scatter fruit
Throughout the world,—and so her sisters thought.
But pity 'tis to tell, she had not learned
Her text; confounded rights and wrongs, and mixed
With them base licenses. Unhappy choice
Of women earnest in their cause! She brought
Upon their work a stain, and ruin marked
Her course like worm-corroding path that blasts
The rose. But we anticipate our tale;—
She begged to speak, for she had come to bring

To them a moral freedom. Right to live
Outside the code that serves to bind our hearts
To clay that holds no soul.
    "I beg you look,"
She said, "at yonder marriage bond, she dreams
Of love that brings no care, so pure her heart,
That life whose aim is solely reaching forth
For wealth, jars rudely heart strings tuned to high
And lofty anthems of the soul, yet finds
Herself beside a mate who soars in thought
No higher than his farm, his plough, his grain
And corn! Her heart that yearns for infinite joy
With kindred souls, by this fell weight here forced
To grope and mourn the unattainable.
And here we find another hapless pair.
To fashion's wheel the wife is bound, and up
And down the giddy world she's whirled, first here
Then there, a ceaseless round no soul-life wakes
Nor genius germ, nor ideal worth. Alone

He stands, the problem of progressive worlds
To solve; looked on by her, as years do more,
And more the breach make, wide, as but a clod
Of earth, that knows not how to grace a feast
Or turn retort in fashion's banter, nor
To dance a reel when most she wished to show
Her gown and shake beneath the nose of gossipers
(For politic she too can be at times)—
Her matrimonial chains to make them talk
Of conjugal felicity and her.
"Arise, my friends! Here have you builded you
A mimic world; throw off as well, the chains
That make you still as worldly here as those
Who live without, and bow to fashion's code.
Affinities must guide you here. Divide
These lives that, tied here side by side, without
One common thought, one lofty dream of Heaven
On earth, drag each other down! Move on,
Let not your work cease here. Grasp other truths.

Let love sit by, a guest, who comes to-day,
To-morrow gone; an angel worthy all
Our best and brightest thoughts, for he gives all,
And more in like return of purest love!
Grieve not, when he be gone, its bitterness
By sweets is e'er replaced with eyes grown dear
Through newly wakened sympathies! Grow
    young,
Not dumb to th' emotions of the heart, and thus,
You'll find the plant of love blooms o'er and o'er.
Away with cant of chains that bind; of ring
That holds for good or ill! Can dead hearts beat
Response to yours? Dull brains give ans'ring
    thoughts?
Ah no! and marriage bonds kill first the one,
And—"Stop"—and Evelyn Grant, in righteous
    wrath,
Stood up and faced the woman who had dared
Invade this realm of peace. "'Tis plain you mean

By love, a word too base to use at large.
That lust can satisfy a heart like yours
I will allow.   Has mother heart ne'er beat
To hush in sacred calm your passion's flame?
Has love ne'er caused you measure which was best,
Love dragged a day in lustful pleasures, or
Th' affections which doth follow it when held
As something sacred for a life?   Or is it
That you have so dull an intellect
That chasteness, and affectionate calm, respect
Of man, because you are a woman born,
Ne'er reached your dimmed perceptions.   Still
  I say!"
For here the stranger tried to speak, but paled
To feel the electric thrill of eyes that looked
Her down in scathing scorn, as on she sped
In quick rebuke.   "Who taught you first to
  breathe

Your infant prayer? Would you have learned had not
It been ordained that those who walk before
In this advancing life, should aid to wake
To life and action, mind and heart, and soul;
Should strive to gain from those who stand below
An upward glance, or more; an upward step?
All selfishly you seek for kindred souls,
'Affinities,' in your weak reasoning,
Content alone to feast while leaving those
You ought to feed, to starve for moral aid.
Ask duty, not the whim of passing hour,
What are most meet for proper wedlock here.
It is divine, the marriage law, what though
Mistakes are made, does that still prove the law
At fault? The wife who dreams the livelong day
What better balance to her vagaries,
Than sturdy sense of what you deem so dull?
Is sense or judgment, then, beneath in grade,

To longings vain, to sophistries of which
She may herself be all too ignorant?
And he, the dreamer that you pity, linked
To wife who worships fashion and the world,
Has he not err'd in closing, oyster-like,
Within himself the pearls of loftier aims?
Let him concede to dwell with her within
The world, join in her pleasures, there to learn
The broader meanings—Charity at home
Begins, and give, instead of holding back
What he considers wealth—and she but dross,
Till each, and both do borrow light, and lend
Until they're harmonized to perfect whole.
And then the little ones.   Must they be plunged
In chaos of these mix'd affections too?
Ne'er cling to anchors such as sacred name
Of mother, father, what though parents these,
'Midst cares too great for poverty to ease,
They lose, perhaps, sublimity in life.

Shall not of life the simple attributes
Which wealth or learning ne'er can give or take
The patient word, the tender hand, the smiles,
The tears, shall these not all suffice to bring,
While moving onward, all that life to live
Is worth and make of wedded life the calm
And steadfast haven of our earthly bliss?
Who talks of else, hath wrought a curse upon
Themselves by marriages not made in love,
But only through some worldly thought; some chance
Or worse, unholy passion's end. Oh, friends!
If, as of old, the serpents crept within
Our Eden here, at least let each of home
Conserve an Eden still."
      The meeting closed.
And deeply entered words like these in hearts
Of most. But some there were who sought excuse
To free themselves from chains they wore but ill,

Who raised contentions till the worst was done.
Midst other homes on which the evil fell,
Was that of gentle Evelyn, who saw
And wept to see the ruin that was wrought,
For stone by stone the edifice man's hand
Had raised, the social ramparts which on earth
Were meant to guard the tender growth of good,
Now crumbled to the dust. What man had spent
Of worldly wealth to aid in this good work,
Was sacrificed, or else they needs must cling
To codes in which they could no more believe.
And yet she held with steadfast soul to truths
She felt must live for aye. But Andrew smiled,
And sighed, and then he smiled again. He dwelt
Where poets dwell; dreamed dreams, nor lent his
    pow'rs
To uses that the practical might win,
When dreams with gauzy fabric, served alone
To dim the clearness of the inward sight

In sense and judgment, when a need like this
Arose for firm and steadfast will. He vowed
Or rather hinted that he lived for aims
Above the toil and sweat of brow which brought
But pelf, wrote letters filled with verse, and vain
Imaginings to lady friends, and then
Felt hurt when answer never came to them.
He hinted in them, life was all a sad
Mistake to spirits that, like him, ne'er found
A kindred soul. None understood his heart,
Nor realized how fiercely burned the fire
Upon the sacred altar of his long
Unsatisfied desire to worship here,
Alone the true and beautiful.
       His wife
Was strong, made brave by mother love. Scarce
  thought
Of strifes begun with worldly wealth all gone.
With her such love gave pow'r, to him it was

But dreaming, and to leave the haven where
He hoped to live and die, meant life begun
Anew, with all the cares of age, and lost
The hopes of youth. She lived anew her youth
In each young life God gave her right to call
Her own. He loved them all, but only from
Their youth had borrowed timorous fears, he
    thought,
And argued o'er and o'er the case, and thus
With others in the vale, in argument fond,
Drank ever deeper draughts to wake and warm
The blood to heat of the debate, talked on,
Nor thought of work that must be done to save
These mouths from need of food.
                          Ere long it came
To pass that it was whispered through the town
That Andrew's head was turned. At least 'twas
    true
That once or twice some fiery drink had ruled

His brain, and scenes arose that made him seem,
If not insane, a man not quite himself.
He walked about the town in strange attire;
Or strayed away for days.

                There sometimes came
To Evelyn, in absences like these,
A stranger, from some neighboring town and bent
On curious errand he, perhaps to claim
A bureau which her husband sold. "Would she
Be kind enough to point him out the one?"
At other times it was a chair, or bed,
And Evelyn with dignity complied,
Nor chose to show to stranger's eyes, she had
Not known, and countenanced their sale. At last
One called to see the clock, a farmer he,
And broad in English dialect. The clock!
'Twas all that spoke to her of girlhood's home.
Her father's gentle voice had mingled with
Its chimes! Each hour it tolled brought memory

Of lessons learned from him!

     "The rare old clock!
The Scots had aye an love for them, but bless
The 'oman, do ye weep? Its awkwarder
Nor what I thought!" And helplessly he scraped
His rough, gray chin,

    "A bit of gold is worth
The clock, but blamed if I can buy the tears.
I thought the feyther needed gold, but 'ems
As sell the meyther's heart, 'ull come to grief!"
"Nae, nae, ye munna mind," and Evelyn,
Her pain too great to mark her words, spoke too
In dialect her father used, and then,
Remembering herself, she sadly smiled,
To see the children marvel at her Scotch.
"The clock, I'm sure, is safe with you, and when
My babe,"—and here the tears choked back the
  words
An instant, while she drew her Edalaine

Against her heart—" When Edalaine is grown,
I'm sure you'll sell it back to her, for o'er
Its face has chased the sunshine and the cloud
Of all my life. Its only silences
Have marked the greatest changes of my days.
Three months to sail from Scotland, was the first.
Eleven years I numbered then, and now"—
She spoke as if the others were forgot,—
" At twenty-two my father gone, and I
A bride, it paused but half an hour when moved
To humbler home than e'er it yet had known.
At thirty-three, for Andrew loved to roam,
We left Canadian soil, and I, my kin.
At forty-four we joined the Fourierites,
And now"—and when she looked at him he marked
The wanness of her face, as if some grief
Had been revealed to her in cruel haste,
Or waked to conscious knowledge of itself,—
" I feel 'twere best, that of my life, the clock

Should never know the rest, lest he, who loved
My youth and called me daughter, yet can look
Upon its face, and still thereon might read
More truth than wittingly I'd have him know.
'Tis folly, is it not? But more through that
Rude clock my father speaks to me, than aught
On earth, and, absent from my sight, I'd feel
My ills can better hide themselves from him."

             The man
Had busied himself in gazing at the clock,
Had oft his cotton handkerchief drawn forth
Or taken snuff to hide his tenderness
Of heart. And now he beckoned Edalaine.
" And so it be, yere Scotch, my gell," he said,
"That's maist as good as bein' Lancashire.
An' when yer grow'd we'll see what says the clock
Of gells as minds their meythers, an' their books."
But Edalaine crept back to touch the face,
All wet with falling tears, and whispered her

In one word: "Mother," all the sympathy
And love an aching heart could wish. The dame,
As if aroused to dearth of duty done
In hospitality, beneath her roof,
Arose and briskly set about the task
Of making tea.
        "I beg your pardon, sir,
My lack of courtesy, you'll take with us
A cup of tea? You see of late our work
Hath fallen slack. The Fourierites could not
Break faith without its shadows falling on
Us all, and since we ceased to break our bread
In peace around one board, we've lost, I think,
Our skill, perhaps 'twas wrong to so withdraw,
But since mine ears were shocked with converse
    filled
With poisonous intent to minds, I felt,
With all my little ones, 'twere best contend

With bitter want; face sickness, nay, meet death,
Than taint their minds with foul disorders which
Now brood within our midst."

"Well said," good dame;
If aught goes wrong, yer welcome to my best,
And there's th' wife o' mine 'ull say the same,
Send me the gells ye need the least, and so
It pleases ye, they'll allays hev a home."
And so the clock was borne away, to leave
With Evelyn a greater grief than she
Had shown, for still, in painful silence, mused
She o'er the strange demeanor of her once
"Guid mon."

Sometimes, as mother with her child,
She strove to reason with and bring him back
To calm and steadfast purposes of toil.
"There's naught in such

A life. I've done thy way

Now leave me to my own." "But, father, think!"
"Aye, aye, 'tis think, 'twere better that I ne'er
Did think!" And while the mother hid her tears,
And yielded task she felt a useless one,
He'd next, perhaps, arouse her latent hopes.
But hopes thus waked would languish when his work
By freaks of fancy moved. 'Twas first to plant
A cherry tree beside the door, and joy
Awoke as cheerful converse then they held,
While he in earnest work with spade delved on,
And she, with needles clicked the stitches off
And on; but next her heart sank hopelessly.
He left the work of usefulness to roam
To distant spot, and paused, perhaps, beside
The brook, to plant what marked in after years
The strange caprice of wand'ring mind. "They'll stand,
Babe Edalaine, to speak to thee of thy

Poor father's deeds in fairer language than
The world will do."

    And Evelyn would say
Unto her flock:

    "Respect thy sire, he soon
Will be himself, his losses make him seem
Unmindful of thy wants. Take heart and do
Thy duties each." But most she strove to make
His acts appear both natural and right,
And they, the children, seldom saw in him
A strangeness, sole, that oft he quitted work,
Nor came to mark the hour of bright-eyed noon,
Or sun's decline, as once he never failed
To do, but lingered late, or never came
At all, though mother ever found excuse.

  * * * * * * *

'Midst all the agitations of belief
Within the vale, and changes brought by them,
Death came again to gather home a soul,

And left Dean Brent to mourn his gentle wife.
He bowed before the grief as strong men do,
And hid his wound afar from careless eye
Of men.   It seemed but yesterday since they
Were wed, but years could ne'er bring back as much
Of quiet joy as marked these peaceful months.
And yet he sought with philosophic mind,
To gain some little good where most the lash
Of sorrow touched to quick the quivering soul.
Elizabeth, such comfort could not find.
She walked the earth as in a misty world
Of blighted joys, and duties which she took
Upon herself with earnest wish, she did
In slow, lethargic wise, as if her soul
Refused to lighten irksome labor with
Impulsiveness.   The springing step, the smile
That mocked the sun, the glow of sun-lit eyes,
Were gone.   Her only sign of interest

In life was shown at times to Edalaine,
Who, child as yet, still read the sadness writ
Upon her sister's face, and crept full oft
Within her arms to nestle there, and lend
A silent sympathy more deep than words.
Dean Brent amidst the sorrows of his own
Sad hearth, who saw his mother fading fast,
Found time to prove to Mistress Evelyn
The worthiness and high esteem he felt
For her, and tried some goodly seed to sow
In mind of Andrew. Sought in outward things
To raise some interest, as ballast this,
To vagaries he feared e'en more than yet
Confessed to idle gossipers. He urged
Some measures to retrieve his fortune lost,
And staked his own in urging this, to feel
At last some hope that all was well. Then signs
Of strange and fitful vagaries again

Appeared, and these more startling proved to
    them,
When late one night, returned from fierce debate,
He sprang with dreadful oaths upon his child
Elizabeth. Her blood congealed in veins
Of ice, she could not scream, but given power
To move, she fled across the Common, 'neath
The stars, without a thought of whence her aid
Might come, and saw alone athwart the night,
The gleam of hungry steel, and felt herself
The object of a maniac's hate, and he
Her sire!
    At last a glimmering ray of light
Fell straggling down a narrow wooden stair.
She heard the grate of heels in hot pursuit,
The pant of rage, and as she touched the stair,
The muttered oath seemed close, so close she felt
Hot breath upon her cheek, and shrank against
The shaded side!

              Come hope! Come help! Alas,
A hand is on her hair, the knife is raised,
And roused to superhuman effort, shrieked,
"Help! help!" When falling at the feet of two
Strong neighbor lads. An instant more, the knife
Is wrenched away, and Andrew strongly bound.
But all that night and many more, when safe
'Twixt prison walls in lieu of hospital,
He raved with incoherent phrase, and when
Some questioned why this awful deed he sought
To do, he answered proudly, while he showed
Upon the wall, a hand which grasped the world,
And which with hasty stroke his hand had drawn,
"Hush, am I not the great I Am? Why ask
Me then of deeds performed, for as I gave
I take, so question none!"
                         For months he lay
In prison chains, nor wife nor faithful friends
Had means or pow'r to save him this. His mind

Took flight in fancies that when spoken, seemed
The words of one whose wisdom was above
The ken of common men, and not of one
Whose mind had lost its equipoise.
        At last
Set free he walked abroad to meet the sun
Of spring. The past forgotten, sane he seemed,
And kindlier man in all the land could not
Be found. Long hours he spent in solitude;
All nature's creatures followed him, nor turned
Away unnoticed. Shy at first, the boys
Found he could make their whistles best, could fly
A kite that failed all other hands, till last
Not few but all the children made of him
Their confidant, and spent full many a day
In climbing through the glens, in weaving flowers
For wreaths, while he wove words in fairy tales,
For Andrew had a poet's heart, and they
Had each a heart of youth, and youth to those

Who understand is much akin to realm
Of poet, save in giving speech to joys.
Two hearts there were that could not thus forget
The past, and both in secret bore a heart
Of fear unknown to each and to the world:
Elizabeth and Edalaine.   And oft
Elizabeth awoke at night with brow
All moist with fright in dreaming o'er the grief
And horror of that awful night.   The child,
By nature born discreet, had never told
That she had waked to see the self-same night,
Her own life menaced by a chair which fell
Upon her mother's form, who strove to save
Her sleeping child; nor how she silent lay
In trembling fear, to hear her mother's voice
(The father fled) thank God in grateful prayer
That he had saved her child from certain death.
And now that all was past, and by the world
Forgot, the terror lived within their hearts,

Increased the more by secret watchfulness.
Yet he was happy, seemingly, nor felt
Estrangement in these gentle hearts.   His life
Was spent in sunny idleness, the lads
Aye glad to find a nobler head to lead
The van in rambling through the summer woods,
With acclamations, hailed a sunny day
Proposed by Andrew for another jaunt.

    One day, when resting 'neath the forest trees,
With twenty merry lads about his knee,
He told in rambling rhyme, the following tale
Of ocean shell:

  I'm shaggy and brown and rough to see,
    As imbedded I lie in the mere;
  The maids would scoff in merry glee,
    If you named me as their peer.

  I'm shaggy and brown and rough, they say,
    In my weather-stained house so round,

But its hall within's a shimmering way,
    That thrills with an echoing sound.

My pearl walls sing songs they cannot hear,
    Gleam with lights they never can see,
For once the ocean in secret here,
    Gave the song of his heart to me.

We sing of his joys the livelong day,
    And sometimes we whisper a sigh;
I'm joined to my wall like moss to clay,
    And we are one, my wall and I.

Yet sometimes, alas, for flesh am I,
    I dream of and long for fleshy kind;
I would they might feel these songs pulse high,
    Through the heart, the brain and mind.

I dream, too, oft of a song I hear,
    From a mermaid sad, though sweet and fair,
Who grievously tried, to sigh, sits near,
    While she sings away her care.

Edalaine.

Only a bubble of ocean am I,
  Alone, alone,
    Alone to moan,
      Alone to die.

My true love went, but he comes not yet,
  Alone, alone,
    To make sad moan,
      With eyelids wet.

I comb my hair beneath the briny deep,
  Alone, alone,
    To make my moan,
      Alone to weep!

He comes no more, and he sends no word,
  Alone, alone!
    Alone to die,
      My prayer unheard.

    Then Andrew told
A tale of storms that rose in foamy rage,

When sea gods 'twixt themselves made war for
    right
To rule beneath the sea. Then ocean stern,
With visage dark, the chamberlain of his court
Bade go, and herald out the powers of all
The Storm King's mighty court, his legions vast,
To work the bane of those who had disgraced
The sea. "What though," he said, "I banish all
From out this wide domain, I'll not submit
That we, like human beasts, get right by might.
Go forth and make it known to them, that ne'er
Again, 'neath surf or wave, shall they as nymphs
Disport, but grovel 'neath the form of man,
Their cares all know, their weal, their woe, and
    make
Of life one constant wage of war for pelf,
Or fame, a struggle fierce, as it shall be
Unending, where I shall not reign their King."
The Storm King came, the storm arose to drive

Them from the sea, and sinless ones like those
Of guilt, were cast upon the barren shore.
The shell whose lonely life we know, like these
Was cast on burning rocks, and wak'd but half
To conscious things, first found himself alone,
And then—but let him tell the tale himself.
"I woke convulsed with pain. A burning heat
Consumed my frame, and thirst my tongue clave
 fast ;
A fiery light ne'er seen before, my brain
And senses scorched. No sheltering home above
My head, for half and half my hall was cleft,
And I, on sands that stretched afar, lay fixed
Betwixt two rocks. I moaning raised my eyes,
When lo ! the light grew soft and dim with tints
Of ocean green. Above, long streamed fine threads
Of silky hair, that dripped like tinkling rain,
Refreshing showers upon my face, as from
The depths it came, and lo, my mermaid queen,

Whose song I long had heard, with tender looks
Bent o'er my head, to know if I still lived.
"Who knows," she murmured, sweetly sad, "might not
This be my love, perchance these troublous times
Changed quite to form and shape like this?" and sought
To give me aid. When all at once, the light,
(I heard them call it sun) with sudden sweep
Was hid. Deep night it was, and then 'twas day,
But weird and frightful day, that scarce had come,
When night more deep, more dense and weird returned.
Reverberations swift of thunders vast,
Had deafened all the land, when I uprose,
To feel some new-born form had compassed me.
"The curse, the curse!" the mermaid cried, and reached

Her arms to meet my own encircling ones.
The curse it was, but joy to me. One form
Were we, of stature just, a man and maid
Become! My heart beat high, I thought not lost
My peace beneath the sea, but linked with her,
What curse would I not dare to live beneath!
She called me "Love," and I, who loved in truth,
Yet let her dream that I indeed was he
She mourned beneath the sea in mournful song.
The fearful storm that gave us birth, passed by,
And nature, who convulsively brought change,
Once more returned to calm. Not so my heart.
It beat the passion music of my soul,
Forever tuned to strike harmonious chords
In unison with hers. Harmonious
They were, for o'er and o'er we sounded still
The rhythm of our love's soft cadences.
Soft, sad, loud, long, nor ever dreamed to know
A weariness of them!

Her mermaid life
Had been an idle, careless one, nor bird,
Nor bee upon the wing, so free as she!
But now she toiled, and oft I wondering sat
To see the busy hands at household task.
In time was added unto us a child,
Nay, two and three, and mother-heart uprose
In her, and I was left apart, as one
Less dear, or so in jealous mood I thought.
Then friends were made. They came beguil'd by
    grace
Of my fair wife. And more and more each day,
As led by jealous fears and pride, I sought
To hide from her my heart, I sank into
Myself. I mourned again my ocean life.
For harmonies that first bewitched this life
As man, in jangling discords lay. And thus
Again I turned to still the venom'd sting
That ate my heart, to dwell on sounds till now

Almost forgot, through charm of blissful love,
To hymning of my shell I turned, but this
Tuned not so full. Its vibratory round,
Alas, rent quite in twain, rang not to me
With even beat, and so led me astray.
When sometimes I, half pitiful for those
That heard it not, th' interpretation sought
Full oft to make their understanding meet.
"He's mad," they said, "with this his broken
    song,
Heed not," to wife, and she ofttimes would weep.
Then I'd give o'er and dream alone, yet knew
She watched me closely, reading random words
As fancy wrought upon, and heeded not.
To see and feel this, day by day, like foul
Suspicion's sting, wrought poison in each nerve,
Till, madden'd, often to my heart I cried:
"'Tis worse than death, my life indeed is cursed."
Sometimes I turned in anger on my young,

As they who brought me ill. Sometimes on her
I loved above all life, or future day.
And once, alas, that I should live to tell
The shameful tale,"—

                 Just here, from far to East,
A bell pealed forth the noon-day hour with loud
And merry chime, that reached e'en to the wood
Where Andrew sat, 'midst listening lads, his tale
Full long to tell.

                "Enough, enough!" he cried,
"The rest will wait our lunch, so bring it forth
And we will feast, while he our hero mourns
Another hour his wrongs, and then we'll leave
These wreaths aloft, a temple raised for him,
To serve as memory of his doom; a day
To live, a day to die, an emblem fit
Of joys."

            And no mean lunch 'neath oaken tree

Was spread upon the ground. Eggs, opened through
Their orange hearts, on couch of lettuce crisp
Nor touched as yet by wine made sharp by aid
Of heat and air, and Andrew, as he turned
It out:

"We often say of one: he sour'd,
Look, boys, a lesson learn, that all in life
Has use, and so with man, the strong keen edge
Of life's wine, turned by adverse winds or heat
Of burning fires, to vinegar, so called;
Has much of use, as when his life ran wine
A ruddy stream. Remember, then, for this
I think you all can understand, to seek
The difference 'twixt a wine that's simply sour'd,
And one that's worked itself full clear like this.
In man, whose nature sour'd would still have use,
You'll find the difference is, to stand above
The dregs, Despair, with Courage fix'd on brow

And heart; to mingle with the pure and good,
Who lend sweet grace of Heaven."

       Thus Andrew talked
At moments, more to self than them, and still
Prepared the meal; cut down with even stroke
The bread of snowy, crumbly textur'd form;
A million bubbles kneaded down, then set
To rise again in finer texture still,
And then, by heat caught fast and welded thus,
In snowy piles with oaken tinted frame
Of bubbles deftly brown'd.

      As Andrew from
The baskets laid, of chickens, pies, of fruits
Full store, the elder boys a fire of pine
Beneath the kettle made, for even this
Was not forgot to make their meal a feast.
And fumes of coffee soon arose, a King
Could scarce withstand had he recorded vows
To keep the day a solemn fast.

A new
Freak this, of their old friend to bring a lunch
With them, and so, the viands spread around,
A glorious feast they make, as gladsome lads
And merry bent as ever plunged in wood.
The eating done, he sent them forth in quest
Of ferns, and buds, and flowers, and all the wealth
Of growing grace, "while I the while will take,"
He said, "a noon-day nap to mend my wits.
And when I wake I'll make resound like this,
The woods;" and straightway with his hands up-
    raised,
A mocking blast of hunting horn with skill
The echoes of the wood awoke.
                             So off
They troop with merry laugh, with shout and
    song,
To leave him there alone. "How still the woods,

Their voices gone! The leaves themselves droop
    one
By one, the bird has ceased his song! Alone!
So like my life, alone to live, alone
In silence ever! Hearts I call mine own
Wake not the silence of my soul by their
Responsive thrills. Unknown to them I am
But mad! Why seek the error to dispel?
I'm mad, aye mad! 'Twere better then to be
Insane, than such blind fools as they." And so
He mused as swinging through the boughs he wove
In graceful fashion, wreaths the boys had made,
Till o'er him swung a fairy bower well worth
A wood nymph queen.
                      He threw himself upon
The sward which rose into a mound, half closed
His eyes, or upward glanced with slanting lids,
To rest the flight of sight amidst the chains
Of trembling flowers. Full long he gazed, for they

Were fair, of every hue, and shape, till soon
They seemed to bend toward him, to nod and then
To smile. Their leaves seem'd wings that gently
    swung
To rhythm of their song. Their stems took shape
Of fairy feet that twinkled in the sun.
And all at once a thousand lips to words
Like these broke forth in sounds of ecstacy:

    Come up, come up,
    Oh, world-worn soul,
    For we are queens of the air.
    Come up, come up,
    And be our king,
    Thou art great and we are fair

    Hither, come hither,
    We'll bear thee up,
    To thy soul we are akin.
    Hither, come hither,

> To be our king,
> For the great and fair are twin.

The sun peeped down to touch the sward where
    lay
With misty eyes, the stalwart frame of him
That heard the song. A handsome form, a head
Of noble shape, with rich brown hair that clung
In rings close link'd. A shapely hand he raised
In sport to shake negation, then in words:
"Ah no, my friends! 'Tis true I wove my life
In web of fairy texture, told my griefs
To ease my heart, while telling tales to please
The lads, but then, no credence give to you
That woo me hither, tho' I oft would flee
The weary ills, the lingering grief that life
Doth prove to me." And they with song chimed in:

> Hither, come hither,
> You'll learn our worth,

Sole when we dwell together.
Hither, come hither,
We're one with thee,
We'll hold thee our king forever!

And Andrew started, drew his hand across
His eyes, as if to brush away a sight
He could not full believe, to prove himself
In dreams. But still the voices rose and fell
In treble shrill, or sank to whisperings.
"I dream," and then he struck his hand against
A root, to prove himself awake, and drops
Of blood oozed through the tender skin, and stood
Like crimson-coated sentinels, that warn
Life's foes 'gainst rude or hasty entrance through
The portals of his palace. Then he rose
And gazed with wilder eyes. The drops had turned
To millions, and they seemed to bear the light
Of scorching mid-day sun! Again he struck
The root, and shrilly laughed to feel the pain.

"Sting me, demons, sting me, one and all,
I'll conquer yet." And then a sudden pause,
As if a thought had stayed his hand. "My God!
Is't madness?" Then he muttered, "Ho ho, I'm
    mad!
I'm mad, am I? We'll see, we'll see!" and lashed
To fury by accusing, unseen foe,
He seized a sapling, tore it from its roots,
And then another, and a third, until
His lacerated hands left witnesses
Of tortured flesh upon each tree.
                                At last,
His fury spent, he sank upon the knoll:
"I'll conquer them, the demons, see!" and held
Aloft the saplings, stripped of bud and leaf.
The flowers bent down their graceful heads; the
    breeze
Sighed softly through the trees; a bird came nigh
Then fluttered through the bower above his head,

And panting, bleeding, passion-pale he lay
And turned his restless eyes to flowers he had
Addressed. Again they nodded in his sight,
And once again their voices caught his ear:

>Hither, come hither,
>Nor mock despair,
>For we wait to crown thee king.
>Hither, come hither,
>And sport with us,
>Oh, trust thy weight to our wing.

>Come up, come up,
>Oh, world-tossed soul,
>And sport with us in the air.
>Come up, come up,
>Oh, world-wise king,
>Thou art great and we are fair.

The pallor deepened on his brow, his eyes

Grew sombre as he listened to the words,
And now forgetting still to answer them,
He saw them nearer, nearer come, till they
Had bent so low, their wings caressed his face.
Their breath bedewed his brow, and still he gazed
With eyes dilated in their disk of blue,
Till arms of fairy forms, of endless hues
Outstretched encircled him. Then all was dark

  * * * * * *

Deep in the woods the boys had met to fight
A mimic tournament, and crowned with flowers
The victor lad; when through the woods some said
They heard friend Andrew call with thrilling sound
Of horn. Some said it was the owl's hoarse cry,
In frightened daylight dream. At last, with one
Accord they turned to seek the spot they left
At zenith sun, to weight themselves with flowers.
They spied from far the bower raised, and ran
With speedy steps to cast their sweets of fern

And buds before the temple raised to love.
The first to reach the odorous arch, a shriek
Sent up to Heaven, then turned with wild, white
    face,
To hide his sight in brother's breast, and shake
With fear. Another came, then fled tow'rd home,
Nor stayed to know the worst. The next that
    gazed,
Fell on the grass, while others came to look,
Transfixed with fear. Some huddled silently
Around, or whispered through white lips: "He's
    dead!"
All dropped the flowers beneath the form that
    hung
By ropes of blossoms, till ne'er conscious what
They did, his feet were buried deep in them.
Then, gathering sense of what they shuddering
    viewed
Like frightened deer, when startled at they know

Not what, they sped tow'rd town, nor scarce could
    voice
For fright, fatigue, and tears, the tale which told
The horror which had crown'd the festal day!
Enshrined with fragrant flowers he helped entwine
The dead there lay! Deep shadow fell to
    shroud
In pitying darkness purple hues that marked
A fate as cruel as a felon's death!
His latest born, sweet Edalaine, first taught
Of death by grief it brought a sister's heart,
Now learned of death self-wrought, and longed to
    know
What suicidal death could mean. First longed
With fear, and then with fever'd wish to gaze
Upon the dead. None knew, when crept alone,
Awe-stricken to the silent room, the child,
To stand till childish currents of the heart
Were frozen in their course, by whispered words

She heard from watchers there.
                              "A pity 'tis,
That Edalaine, the babe, was ever born!
For surely she must bear within her veins
The fatal legacy that wrecks the mind,
And soon or late must wake a maniac."
" You think that Edalaine is born to fate
So dire?" " Aye, think I so of Edalaine,
Or that of children she may bear."
                              The child,
No longer child, with white, set face, went out,
And later, asked a neighbor girl to tell
Her what could mean a maniac. The girl
A moment paused, then told the worst she knew,
Told all the word implied, and cited acts
That Edalaine failed not to recognize
As those of her own sire. And yet she seem'd
Unconscious of the likeness drawn, nor spoke
Nor questioned of the girl more than she gave

In voluntary clearance of the first
Demand.   And later, listening to the sound,
As fell the earth into his grave, she gazed,
And whispered to herself without a tear:
"And must I die a maniac?"

BOOK III.

The ling'ring summer passed and like the grace
Lent tree and flowers, so brought to Edalaine
A subtle charm of face and form quite new,
And if one felt her smiles were rarer grown,
And that a touch of sadness lingered there,
She was no less a winning maid that crept,
Before one knew, deep in the hearts of all.
'Midst simple country folk and village ways,
Beloved by all, sweet Edalaine lived much
Within herself, amidst the farmer's maids
Seemed nothing more than they, except to win
The more of love, and yet, unknown to them
And to herself, a spirit emanant

About her, seemed to breathe an atmosphere
Peculiar to herself, now gay, now sad,
And here existence took upon itself,
An ideal beauty all its own,—the trees,
The sunshine, birds and flow'rs, breathed subtle truths,
In language eloquent—they filled her soul
With melodies that sung themselves within
Her heart, in cadences of youthful joy.
From sun-dipped clouds she gathered quiet peace.
The lark woke action crowned with hope and joy,
The dew-kissed daisies, trembling at her feet,
Taught bright humility and cheerfulness,
When patience tried.
    Ah, who that has not lived
Up-borne by poets' dreams, who has not seen
In rock and fern, the air itself, the signs
Of beauty there, knows not of earth one half
Its worth, nor tastes of Heaven its joy!
          The flock

Of Evelyn, of which she was the last,
Had been divided, two had gone to homes
Provided them by loving hearts and hands—
Though over-young to wed, good Evelyn
Had given o'er to pleadings which, at least,
Held better reasoning than she could find
To make delay. Their choice had not been ill.
Two others found a sheltering home with him
Who first foresaw the coming cloud and bade
Dame Evelyn relie on him. His wife
Was thrifty, wise and provident, and taught
Them lessons which they treasured for a life.
And one had gone to teach a village school.
But Edalaine remained, so now their home
Was broken up, Elizabeth had brought
Them home to chase from off her heart the shades
Of memory. Well medicined her heart
From earlier wounds, in minist'ring to those
She loved and with them bearing living grief.

One day, when years had wrapped about her past
Its pitying mantle, like the green of moss
That hides upon a lofty tree the wound
A cruel woodman's axe, or quivering flash
Of lightning which, not near enough to blast
Has cut away some growing limb, one came
Who loved her as a sister ere they each
Had learned the meaning sorrow bears, and begg'd
In noble phrase she'd lay aside her grief,
And wake to earnest love he offered her,
Dean Brent had learned to prize her, with a love
Not born in haste and sued for its return.
She paled in quick dismay in answ'ring him,
She had not dreamed that he could think of her
In such a way. 'Twas wrong perhaps, she loved
Him more than she had dreamed, she owned, but
      too
She saw her mother fading day by day,
The toil and care, the grief and pain had done

Their work. "Too soon, alas, we'll mourn her loss,
And then, I still must live for Edalaine.
I feel within myself, life holds for her
A work outside the routine of the lives
We all have led, and I would be her shield
And spare her useless struggles she would meet."
"But think you, then, without the ills, one learns
So well their power, their breadth of intellect?"
"'Tis like, some minds do not, but one so keen
To feel the ills, so quick to read the hearts
Of men, can rise to highest plains of thoughts.
Can wisdom gain—of life can know its best
And worst, while seeing more and living less
Of pain."
  "And so you think it wise to spare
Your sister griefs, and shield from her of life
Its tragedies?—"
  "Ah me, I think her life
Was born a tragedy, and I foresee

Alone in occupation sure escape
From conscious knowledge on her part of this."
"But why, Elizabeth, could we not wed,
Could you not trust to me a tithe of this,
Your self-imposéd task?" "Nay, nay, good friend,
You do not understand. Your own desires
Impel you toward a higher work and aim
Than here you'll find; how then can I be yours
And follow you without neglecting them?

"I'll stay, Elizabeth; the sacrifice
Would still be small!"

"And trammel intellect
To gain a wife? Nay, nay, my friend, be wise;
The aspirations crushed for lesser joys
Undo the higher meanings of our lives;
Such wish, such love, is beautiful as true,
But once we find within ourselves some way
To lofty thoughts or deeds—first do our best;
Then comes—if such our fortune's kind decree—

Some recompense in homely joys of life."

"Elizabeth, you shame my weaker heart
With lofty reasoning!"—but still he sought
In phrase of deep impassioned love to gain
Some hope of hither-coming days of joy.
"I pray you cease, dear friend," she said at last;
"Divided hearts can do no perfect work.
Inevitable choice be ours. The sting
Of severance will afford a better spur
Than idle wishes to complete the task
That may demand our lifetime."

        So it was
That he with aching heart had ceased his suit,
And now had toiled three years in foreign lands.
And Edalaine dreamed not of sacrifice
So nobly made in her behalf. Her mind
Engrossed in study, days were all too short;
And when, escaped from school, what dreams were
  hers!

Not those of other girls, but hopeful dreams
Of future usefulness, a life outside
Herself; and so she seemed to live all joys;
The joys of love and innocent delights,
Of youth, and girlhood, seemed to her but gifts
That soon must pass from out her life; nor yet
Was this a painful thought.

      "My days," she said,
"Shall be so filled with care for others that,
I scarce shall know my own has griefs or need
Of sympathy." She never dreamed that years
Might bring her happiness untold; too deep,
The shade of others' sorrows marked her heart;
She only sought to find some solace 'midst
A life of heavy cares. Her cheerful heart
Made no demands, and caught each passing ray
Of pleasure as a blessing sent.

        At last
The routine of her school-days reached their end,

The days in which to choose a fitting path
In life, or failing, live to toil and drudge.
Not only now had thoughts of this grave choice
Waked in her mind, for she had dreamed betwixt
The pages of her books, and each new dream
Took shape again in one that lured her most.
Long time had lived the thought, when late one night,
As seated near Elizabeth, she spoke.
For many moments both had watch'd the shapes
Of ruddy embers glow and fall, and each
Had added fancies to their shape.
                              " I fear,"
The younger said, " the ambition that I prize
Above all others, dear, will disappoint
Your heart ; for surely rumors of the world,
Which, prejudic'd, oft reach us here, have sown
Their seed within your mind as well as that
Of simpler folk. I'd spare you this, but still

In you I know that reason governs more
Than aught of idle prejudice could do,
Or narrow-minded rule.—I ask you then,
My sister, tell me if you think it right
To stifle in our hearts the brave response
Of those emotions deep and grand, that like
The sweep of ocean wave, surge through the soul
When waked by magic touch of nature's truths
Or human woes we see in daily life?
Some men there are who crush emotions back
Upon the heart till naught that's pure remains
To quicken pulse, or waken in the soul
A sympathetic chord of quick response.
The world's becoming dead in soul, when hearts
Should echo each to each like harps well tuned;
Each joy be doubled by the changes rung,—
Our sadness meet a softened gleam of hope,
Through sympathy with those who greater griefs
Have known.   And so, dear, be not grieved that I

Confess I feel that nothing could my days
More nobly occupy than touching, on
The mimic stage of life, the hearts of men,
To bid them see in imitations just,
The tragic woes of men, wherein the griefs
Of others match their own at last; since things
We look upon leave more impress than those
We read. Some hearts, mayhap, unused to woes,
Will thus be stirred from out the sluggish depths
Of pleasures vain, to turn and think,—be moved
To somewhat more intense of daily life,
Than parrot-like to copy sole the weak
And listless routine of a life we know
To lux'ries given."

                        "Think you then, my child,
The stage so nobly plann'd to work out good,
Not ill instead? We have been taught in spite
Of all the breadth of thought our elders claimed
The stage is blame to those who walk its boards."

"All that I know and feel. Who dares to face
The ordeal must live down reproach from those
Who will not follow what I can but deem
Its noble ends."

   "You may be right, my child,
I dare not say,—indeed I could but grieve
To see you choose a life that brings such lures
Of ill—but only promise me to wait
Until we seek advice of those who know
And can advise. I'll write our friend Dean Brent."

  Elizabeth took pen in hand at once
To write the letter, telling him therein,
While touching ne'er upon their past, concise
And clear, her fears and hopes.

       "For aid," she came.
Would he advise her what was best to do?

    A weary waiting 'twas to Edalaine,
The coming word from him who linger'd still
On foreign soil.

"Make no mistake," he wrote.
"Remember this, that while some inward sense,
Some inspiration of the heart doth lead
Our choice in life—if left with us to choose
What best we can fulfill, there's much at stake.
Not inspirations must we trust alone,
But sense of those requirements which are meet
For our success.

    "Say to her this, I beg;
Her noble purpose fills my heart with pride,
And though she failed 'twere nobly done to fail
Through purposes so pure, not pride; but ask
Herself, if well she's weighed the needs within
Herself to bring success. Think not my words
Lack sympathy. The great upon the stage
Must join rare traits of person and of mind;
Presence must lend its charm, the soul its pow'r.
Deep readers of the human mind alone
Can know each phase of life and live them o'er.

Ideal imaginings must weave about
A simple phrase, a world of thought, and wake
A revelation in the hearts of those
Who listen and behold.   Historians they,
To bring before the world its past, in true,
Unsullied spirit of old time.   And here
They need not thought alone, but all the power
Of philosophic minds.—Weigh well the case,
And if of mind the same, let nothing be
Undone to add to talents heaven-born,
The lustre culture only gives.   For this,
Why not risk all, to come abroad where art
Becomes of nature's self the counterfoil,
Why not at least, seek first such paths of life
As may lead surely toward the end in view?
In this maturer world true art matures,
And trusts itself to no such meteor-like
Success as in our land is hailed outright
As heaven-descended genius, but incurs

A speedy fall, or lives by tolerance,—
The mirage where small talents disappear."
    Ambition oft makes exiles of us all,
Or duties which we take upon ourselves,
To Edalaine there seemed no other choice,
Content that others blessed her good intent
It had not long discouraged her to feel
She stood alone with this consent denied.
A month of preparation passed; farewells
With God-speed from a score of friends they go
And side by side upon the steamer's deck,
A week from inland home, the sisters stand
To see their native shore recede from view.
A saddening sight 'twould seem to timid hearts,
But then ambition ever has a wing
That skyward gleams, regardless of the clouds;
And, we must not forget, they bear with them,
A wealth of memories,—the saddest ones
To be through future years a tender joy;

'Twas something sacred to have known their grief;
For grief, when poignant sorrow yields to time,
Exults in new-born strength, although at first
The stricken heart seemed robbed of pow'r to strive.

" I have forgot my past " in vanity
Says he, whose faults like giant ogres haunt
His steps,—" I have no past, it is a blank;
We live but in the present hour; 'tis here
We find our happiness, defeat, or death."
Blind fool! His deeds themselves belie the words.
Why holds he secret enmity toward one,
Or swears revenge the sweetest earthly joy?
What subtle chain now galls, now bids him smile
In sheer contempt of self, that lets a ghost
Of days long past walk side by side with joys
He fain would taste to-day? And why so wide
From what he dream'd in proud and noble youth,
The tenor of his daily life? Alas!

The castle's built, the rampart's raised, and he
With welded chain, lies prisoner within
The walls he built in heedless, reckless haste,
Not dreaming that they needs must stand through-
    out
Eternity itself. And can he boast.
"I have no past—'tis banish'd from my thought?"
But lightly weighs the chain that's worn from choice,
And oft its strength becomes our safeguard when
Our castle's rampart trembles 'neath attack
Of unknown foes.
            And so the sisters turned
With hopeful eyes toward eastern lands, their hearts
Awake to future usefulness, yet sad
With weight of musing that for them, henceforth,
Life would be strange!
              Dame Evelyn, their loved
And gentle mother, slept,—her weary heart
At rest, and yet the lives of both were filled

With presence real and palpable of her;
It was a benediction o'er their lives.

                                      At last they ride
Upon the wave that bears them far from home,
And thoughts of past or future cares are now
Supplanted by the novelty of their days.
The sea an unknown world to them; the ship
A Naiad fleeting between sun and wave,
The care of each; she kisses with wet lips
The god who bears her on his breast.—An isle
It was were minds are brightened to their best
Retort, where soul meets soul without a care
Lest these swift friendships fail the test of time.
Elizabeth ne'er saw her sister's heart
So truly filled with joyousness and mirth;
Her beauty seem'd to gain some added charm,
And brilliant speech to serve as setting rare.
A diplomat, who rarely smiled, perceived
It too, and oft retort waged high between

The two, his sternness melting somewhat 'neath
Her gaily utter'd words whose strength gave sign
Of something deeper than the passing touch
Of lightly uttered repartee, until
He bow'd before her soul-lit eyes with grace
Of pride in thus confessing that his powers
Found match in her.
     To Elizabeth, it was
A revelation marked with grave surprise.
"I dreamed her still a child," she mused; "and yet
She copes with intellects that challenge all
The world!"
    Her voice which, pure and high and clear,
Had often waked the echoes of the hills
At home, rang out in joyous strains uncheck'd
By warning words from tutor'd vocalists,
That voices should not spend themselves upon
The empty space; and so unconsciously
She sang as nature and her soul might prompt.

The shadow of her life was not forgot,
But hopefulness that now her aim would find
Its perfect work had somewhat soothed her pain,
And tears no longer blent their cadence with
Her song; and she herself a happy maid,
Seemed sole inspired to give to others joy.

  At eve one day this diplomat, who seemed
No stranger now, but rather cherished friend,
Said to her gravely, as she ceased her song,
" I glean from what you say, and leave unsaid—
Excuse the seeming freedom of my speech—
That you demand fame of the tragic muse;
Why not make Song instead your life? Unless
Perchance 'tis not yourself you give to art
And aspiration, but caprice alone,
Teasing meanwhile some loving, waiting heart
That yearns, and waits the day the bird will turn,
And seek the cage she now so coyly flees."

  " I then have reached no higher in the esteem

Of Arnold Deith," she said, "than that of weak,
Capricious womankind?"

      "Nay, nay," he said,
"Not that—and yet all that. You are so young,
So joyous and so free from care, I must
Believe you choose a path in art that claims
A life of toil with little recompense
Without a thought of what it may portend;
For certain 'tis, your choice comes not from vain
Desire to claim the empty praise of worlds,
Nor yet from disappointments that lead some
To choose a walk in life where busy scenes
Help them to bury griefs, to hide their woes."

  His earnestness began to move her more
Than merely words he spoke; she felt he sought
To know what lay beneath the gaiety
And mirth; he sought to sting her to retort
By words less just than true.

       " Do none e'er choose
The life you now describe in dread of woes
They feel may come?" she said.
        " In morbid minds
Such dread mayhap may rise—but why should
   thoughts
Like these become a guest in heart so light,
A life so young as yours? What fear can wake
Within your heart the thought that life will prove
Less bright unto the end. It lies with you,
Where'er your fancy leads your heart, to raise
The standard victory, and claim at once
The citadel that sure must yield to powers
Of beauty, youth, and intellect."
        " A truce,"
She cried. "You now drop words of diplomat,
That fall like sounding brass upon the ear,
But lack the soul of truths that reach the heart.
And yet forgive you them I must, since not

Too weak to take offence at raillery,
Or to be hurt when earnest words are deemed
Too deep for puerile natures such as mine."
  "And are you then unconscious of the power
You soon may wield o'er hearts of men," he asked.
"I only know the power that bids me seek
To voice the many conflicts of the heart."
"Ah, then, you are inspired, and will succeed.
But think you not this need you feel may soon
Complete within its counterpart become
When beats your heart response to one belovèd?"
And here he took her hands in his, and gazed
With searching earnestness upon her face.
"I ne'er shall wed," she made reply, "e'en though
I loved. That, then, can never, never be."
And something stern, though sad of voice and
    mien,
Seemed then to check desire to ask her more
And he who never lacked for ready words

Could find no speech.
                    Just then her sister came.
"Dear Edalaine, do sing a good-night song,
The moon is playing hide-and-seek, and soon
Will mark the midnight stroke of bell."
                              "And what
Shall be the song?"   Her voice was strange to him
Who stood in silence at her side, and sent
A thrill of pleasure through that heart, unused
To yield to sudden impulses.   They both
Were moved to something strange,—"The night,"
        he thought,
And she,—"I wish it need not move my heart
To say, I ne'er shall wed—a doom pronounced
E'er danger nears.   I have not loved as yet.
Why need I fear?   And still, O God, I pray,
Remove from me the power to love, and all
Desire."
        Poor child, the need of loving came

E'en with the prayer, as if to mock a heart
That dreamed this life were meant to be a dearth
Of all that's fair to usefulness.
                                She sang,
And never had her voice held half such charm.
She sang as if it respite gave to grief.
Her sister's tears bespoke a wakened past,
Its bitterness and grief, while others felt
The spell that marks ofttimes, in all our lives,
An epoch never more to be forgot.
As died the thrilling notes, she saw alone
The silent form of Arnold Deith, who stood
Apart, and never turned when others spoke.
"Good-night," the others said, and then aroused
From reveries so deep to wake was pain,
He said, " The voice speaks truths the lips would
       fain
" Belie." Then bending o'er her hand, " Beware
Lest griefs too great be yours. The birthright love,

May never be denied. Though passion's strength
Be held in leash. The fiercest storms do come
When nature makes resistance 'gainst itself."
And then, in softer tone, he said, " Good-night."
You'll sing, and hearts will wake to nobler things
Through magic of your voice—" and he was gone.
Yes, she would sing, she felt it so herself,
And wondered at her new and firm resolve.
His words were half command, which she could not
Resist, and would not, if she could ; and then
Besought herself to think more light of one
A stranger still.

                Long hours in wakefulness
That night she lay, then slept, to be disturbed
By phantoms of her childhood fears, that rose
In vivid, fearful forms. She saw again
Her father's death, and heard them say once more

"He's mad,"—and then her dreams more fearful
    grew,
Until the awful dread of all these years
Became a real and hideous truth. She felt
Its dreaded power weight down her every sense;
And, impotent to flee its bane, she cried,
" Alas, 'tis come at last, I'm mad, I'm mad!"
She woke in agony of fright, then slept
To dream again its horrors and dismay.
She dared not sleep a second time again
To feel herself a conscious being, yet
The author of strange deeds that were beyond
Control of will.
            When morning came, she looked
With startled eyes upon the face of those
With whom she spoke, half fearing lest she there
Might read the knowledge that her dreams were
    real
And that her words might soon reveal to them

The strangeness of unsettled mind. She watched
Her words till Arnold Deith in wonder stood,
And said within himself, "How cold she's grown
And proud,—dismayed perhaps because I read
To her somewhat the fires within her soul.
'Tis vain. The fires that smoulder burn no less
The fierce, when adverse winds by chance lay bare
The substance, which they, hidden, hold in bonds
Of glowing, living serfdom. Yes, she thinks
The passions buried ; hearts well veiled are dead.
She aims to be a marble statue, while
She acts in mimic form the real of life
Upon the stage. Nay, nay, 'tis not there lies
Her power, but only that she feel, and lives
To know the depth of soul, the noble pride
That suffers and is strong."

       How far from truth
And yet how near, were musings such as these !
Unconscious of his thoughts, she only fled

Edalaine.

The throng, to teach herself such fears were weak
And brought no good.
                    Sometimes her musings chased
From life its worthiness, and pains she knew
Were meted her seemed heavier weight than she
Could bear, yet singularly she it was
Whose tender joyous face brought smiles and mirth,
Aye, happiness where'er she moved.
                              One morn
Awake at dawn she wandered to the deck
And walked its length, before the sailors came
To flood its planks till, white as snow, they gleam'd
Beneath the glancing sunlight of the day.
Afar a cloud peeped o'er the horizon,
Then gradually unfolded banners white
Of black and white, or glanced in prismic hues,
As it uprose to catch the sun.
                                  Long time
She gazed upon the object, till, amazed,

She walked across the deck and timidly
Aroused the drowsy watchman who, with hand
Upon the wheel, was deep in revery
Or mayhap something nearer sleep.

        "I beg
You, sir," she said, " is that a cloud, or do
We pass so near enchanted land?"

          At first
Surprised he follow'd her and raised his glass
To sweep the broad expanse of sea. The face
Beneath its bronze turned white.

        "Good God defend,"
He cried, "enchanted lands were best, few miles
Away and bearing straight upon us, child.
It is an iceberg!

     Shrill he gave alarm,
And scarce an instant passed till through the ship
The word of danger rang, confused with cries,
And men with stern set faces gazed afar;

Beheld their doom, then turned to battle 'gainst
Swift death.   No holiday diversion this
To stand aside while panoramic fields
Of ice moved by.
    The women came aloft
And huddled 'gainst the cabin.   Many sobbed
Forgotten pray'rs, as toward them came what
  might
Have been a splendid palace meant to bring
Them wondering joy instead of fear.
        Amidst
The agonizéd throng, that only wait
While others work, Elizabeth with calm
And cheerful words moved here and there, now
  spoke
Of hope, and too besought them govern fear
That men might better work to save their lives.
And Edalaine, as if this glittering mass
Had fascinated thus her very soul,

Leaned 'gainst the bulwarks lost in ecstacy
Of sight.
   On, on it came and drove the sea
In fierce gigantic waves that bore aloft
The ship then dropped her down to darkness, while
The towering wave she left, curled o'er to throw
Its lash of bitter brine as if it scoffed
A trivial thing.
   Impenetrably black
The palace seemed, then through some broken niche
A cavern vast of stalactites it shone
With thousand gleaming hues.
     When Edalaine
Was roused by cries about her; roused to sense
Of danger to the ship, she felt annoyed
That life now seemed so small a thing and fear
Held in her heart no place.

                    Once Arnold Deith,
Who paused in passing, drenched himself with
    brine,
Snatched from the deck a shawl which 'round her
    form
He folded close, and so an instant held
Her in convulsive clasp and then was gone
Before her tremor of surprise had passed.
Useless skill of mariner! Though changed
The ship's swift course, yet ever nearer seemed
This moving world that menaced them, and like
A battle from afar whose musketry
Resounded with a deafening round of shot,
So came the chill reverberations, drowned
At times by rushing waves that deluged them
With icy foam, or rocked them in the abyss
Of waves.
         At last above them grandly towered
The frightsome thing, and as they sank, all knew

The coming wave would dash them at its base.
Down, down they sink in furrows of the wave.
All souls not faint with fear, commend themselves
To saving grace; a curious muffled sound,
A shuddering shock; men braced themselves like steel,
And women hid their sight. "We are aground,"
A skipper said, another wave that drove
Them closer, yet they were not freed, nor were
They shattered by the shock. Above them loom'd
The glittering green, and here and there an arm
O'erhung them like a scaffold grim of death.
A fiercer wave, and they were wedged between
A gleaming fissure that an instant might
Suffice to engulph them 'neath a monument
As cruel as 'twas wildly grand. Loud creaked
The frozen raft, and thunders shook the wave
Beneath the ship, and groans like human woes,
From out the glittering caves were borne to them,

Thick shadows fell and it was night before
They dreamed the day begun, though years could not
Efface the eternity of the woe their hearts
Had known. All night the weak ones pray'd, the strong
Could wait on God unsyllabled. Again
The morn uprose and they were drifting south,
A helpless wreck, now held by giant foe
While o'er it swept the lashing wave, enraged
That such a prize be snatched from out their power.
Oft fear, like grief, will know a calm and wake
To strength through borrowed hopefulness. The ship
Imprisoned, bore the onslaught of the waves
With small alarm of ill, the worst was done,
They only drove her firmer 'gainst the ice.
And now in deadly calm they pray and wait

Release that still must be a miracle—
While o'er them hung the cloud uncertainty,
The urgent needs of life demanded food
And this in rations carefully allowed,
And sleep—that first refused to dwell where cries
That seemed the spirit of the damned arose
Where thundering roars and creaking masses rent
The air,—at last crept o'er the grieving hearts.
And like a monody of peace its roar
Swept through their dreams like sweetest lullaby,
A solemn thing it is to daily dwell
With grim, unpitying death, to face the truth
Bereft of every subterfuge. In hearts
Of men such cleansing fires develop traits
That bless them whether life return, or Heaven's
Wide gates unclose to teach them spiritual things.
E'en those that 'gainst the irrevocable
Do battle with unbending will, become
More chastened.

Edalaine these dreary days
Was like a spirit, bringing hopeful joy,
'Twas not the words she said, the hope sh.
    spake,
But resignation that illumined all
Her face with tender joyfulness. "Afraid?"
" 'Tis nature to recoil from pain, but death
When once accepted, more we dread the ills
Of life, be sure its sad uncertainties
Are worse than death."
             The days of anxious dread
Wore on, already they had drifted south
For fourteen days. Meridian suns had spent
Their force in vain to free th' imprisoned ship.
'Twas midnight, and a sudden tempest wak'd
Around the floating continent of ice.
Its ghostly minarets, its towers grand
Stood out like shining marble as the flames
Of lightning swift succeeding each

                                New fear
Clutched human hearts, these souls now used to
        thought
Of death, and scarcely was the danger born
Before a cry of fire was heard.
                            "The boats!"
Vain cry! These once reserved for urgent need
Were useless, wedged between the walls of ice,
A hopeless murmur passed all lips, then ceased,
They now were used to hopelessness—a pause
Succeeded as the flames uprose,—a calm
As if the elements stood still, or held
A consultation with their powerful hosts.
Then mightier thunders rose than mind conceives,
As bolt on bolt the ice king's palace rived
In twain. It parted swiftly, sweeping back
And left the weak, dismantled ship aflame.
Affrighted ones sprang o'er the sides to meet
In waves an enemy less dread than fire.

But Heaven now oped her gates to pour on them,
A deluge that no flame could live beneath,
And rocked between receding cliffs they rose
And fell, till life or death was one to them.
As morning came the waves had quieted,
Yet danger was so near that men who lived
Half envied those whose strife was o'er.

                                        Three days
They drifted, hunger half appeased,—devoured
With thirst,—when joyous cry of " Sails, ho, sails!"
Arose. Strong men grew weak and scarce believed.
A woman, Edalaine, had fainted. Soon
Confirmed, the eager eyes, the haggard cheeks
Were turned to watch for signal, that they came
Indeed to save.

                    What need to follow them?
Some grieved for lost ones, scarcely wishing life,
The rest resigned, now woke again to life,
And brought to it a meaning never known
Before the rod of Might had chastened them.

* * * * * * * *

Two years had looked upon the world, brought
    change,
And left their calendar in hearts of men.
For Edalaine they opened such a wealth
Of lore, such joy of seeking but to find,
They seemed a dream of paradise; bright days
Of sunshine, such as study ever brings
Th' enthusiast, and if at times the fear
Of future ill beset her tender heart,
The thousand occupations of her life
Were sure to dissipate the thought, as oft
The victim of a dire disease forgets
The doom of death.
              Dean Brent, the same old friend
Had made of Paris in these years the field
Of new research, and famed as scientist
He stood among the men whose works had moved
With wonder all the world.

To Edalaine

He came with all his plans for future good
Unto mankind, and she with trustfulness
Into his ear her every secret poured
Except the one,—the hideous nightmare, worse
Than death, which came so oft to mar her peace.
Elizabeth had wondered not to see
These two become so dear. " He has forgot,"
She mused, " and loves again, and so 'tis well.
What man could meet my sister's eyes, and gaze
Therein each day, without impassioned love?"
And then she knelt to pray for blessings on
Their love, and once or twice took from her desk
A faded rose, a letter marked with tears
And after kissing them, stood o'er the grate
Irresolute, for something stayed her hand,
And then once more she hid them in their place.

    One day he sought her side,—" Would speak,"
    he said,

"Of matters which he felt of grave import.
He seemed much moved. Elizabeth, as was
Her wont, was calm and placid, for she knew
Full well of what and whom he meant to speak.
"Elizabeth," he said, " 'tis years since near
The village stream I held your hand and lent
My thoughts to words which found offence to
    heart
So loyal to the living charge. Sweet girl!
She now fulfills, and more, your hopes for her,
And, like your love, has that of mine increased.
I ask of you, Elizabeth, my best
Beloved of friends, what word of words is mine
To bear the one we both do love? Your work
All done, you sure can give her up, or else
Consent that you and I unite in care
Of one we both do love."
                    "Go, say to her,"
Elizabeth replied, with outstretched hands,

"That to your wish, consent I gladly give,
That to this end I daily prayed the Lord.
Not now," she gently said, as he would kiss
Her brow, that paled beneath his look, "not now,
Leave me alone to think,—it is so new,
So sudden come, leave me alone, and go
To her, whilst I compose myself to think
Of dreams so bright, thus joyously fulfilled."
"All mine," he said to Edalaine, who smiled
Through tears, as both her hands he clasped in his.
"Go whisper in your sister's ear what most
Your heart would say. She needs brave words
    from you."
Not loth, she softly tapped upon the door.
No answer came at first, and then she spoke.
"My sister, let me in. You sure will hope
For me your door?" And soon a pallid face
With heavy lids and tear-stained cheeks, had met
Her own.

"And is it then so sad a thing
The being loved?" the younger said.
"Alas,
'Tis giving up thy care," she sadly said,
"Oh, that is naught, indeed, it will not be,
I ne'er shall wed, you know."
"Will ne'er be wed?"
In wonder and amaze the elder asked.
"You ne'er will wed, and still accept the love
That's proffered you?"
"Ah, no, though love there be,
And there are men both good and grand, I ne'er
Must think of love that brings the marriage bond."
"Why, child, what words are these? I fail to read
The meaning they do hide."
And Edalaine,
Love-sheltered in her sister's arms, replied,
"I never thought to tell you this, to grieve

Your noble heart, but since you gave so much
Through love of me—for Dean has told me all
That happened long ago—you now shall hear
The secret of my life." And then she poured
Into her sister's ear the tale of nights
Of torture, grief, and fear that oft beset
Her, spite of reasoning powers and strength of will
At bitter knowledge that to her must fall
The heritage of woe which years ago
Had rendered them both fatherless. She told
The tale that reached her orphaned ears, the words
That burned themselves into her heart and brain.
For her, she learned, must love e'er be a book
Closed sealed, or else must bring but sacrifice,
And yet love stays not hence by force of will.
"You love?" her sister said.
      "Alas, there's one,"
And blushes crept o'er all her face, that looked

A rose that sudden opes its petals wide
At kiss of sun. "I could have loved, I think,
Had bitterness not frightened me for dreams
So sweet. And now, my sister, I would fill
My life with art."
    "And Dean, knows he of this?"
"Why pain the heart of one so kind with griefs
Like mine? 'Twould do no good."
      "And yet 'twere right
To tell him all, for fanciful alarms
Are these, and should be overcome, my child."
"That, as you think, Elizabeth. If so
You choose, I'll tell him all, or leave to you
The task, but let it not cast gloom upon
The brightness of your future life." And then
She left her sister, with a sigh, and sought
 Her books and solitude.
      Her sister knelt,
And wept again. All hope of joy in life

Seemed swept away in knowledge of this loss
To Edalaine.
   "Weak fool, I dreamed to spare
Her all the ills of life; and since a child,
Though walking side by side, we two, the earth,
I never knew the secret grief that wrecks
Her life! Not done my work. 'Tis he perchance
Who yet may teach forgetfulness, may yet
Convince her these are idle fears alone."
A little later, and she nerved herself
To tell to Dean the story she had heard.
"Dear friend," she said, "our Edalaine declares
She ne'er will wed. Forgive me, then, if now,"—
"'Tis ever Edalaine," he said, half vexed.
"I, well, I'm wrong,—you're right, the more my
  love
For you; but if she ne'er will wed, need that
Decrease our happiness?" His hearer gazed,
Her heart stood still, and then a sudden beat

Seemed near to burst its bounds with anger stirred
Her veins to tingle with a flood of fire.
Had he, then too, been tainted with the curse
That fell upon Ceresco's happy vale?
"O Dean, can ears believe such words as these,—
Your happiness? You dare to ask of me
My child to be disgraced by love unblest
By ring or holy wedlock band?"

       "Dare ask
For love? Elizabeth, 'tis I who stand
Amazed! For love unblest by heaven? No,
A thousand times I answer no! *Your* love
I ask,—your hand I beg to bless my life.
Have I so meanly wooed that yet you'd yield
To Edalaine all life, all love, all praise?
O my beloved, let all these years to you
Be witnesses of loyal love. To you
Alone I consecrate my life, and that
Which of your life must be a part."

         And she,
In pallid wonder, struggled with herself.
"But—Edalaine—'twill break her heart. She
  loves—"
Then ceased, as Edalaine before her stood.
"Not brother Dean, dear sister mine," she laid
Her sister's trembling hand in his, then fled
The room to weep for joy.

BOOK IV.

Then marriage bells rang out their joyous chimes
Of hope fulfilled. To Edalaine they brought
A sense of freedom now to merge in art
The abnegation of her love, convinced
That naught could chain her to domestic life.
Elizabeth, her faithful friend, had found
The one to fill her heart with peace and love
All unaware that art would drift the child
She'd nourished long, so far from home and love.
Elizabeth beheld success that step
By step she gained, and was content. She came
And went, and ministered to other hearts
The peace she felt new-born within herself.

Sometimes unheralded on mimic stage
She trod, and 'midst the throng a face awoke
The power to give th' interpretation rare
To song, which marks the narrow line between
The great, and those who never reach beyond
The good,—that touch, that floods the list'ner's soul
With thrills of exultation to exclaim,
"Ah, that is grand, 'tis heart that speaks, not voice!"
At such a time some wondering ones would ask,
" Who may she be that but to-day we hear
Her voice, and hearing her revere the name
Lately unknown to us in art of song?"
While listening to echoes of such praise,
She smiled, and thought, "They do not understand
The art which shrinks from title of itself,
Avoiding undue public praise, is wise;

Lest parts not moulded to a perfect whole
Forget the ideal realm at which they aim,
To bask in idle luxury and vain
Display." Nor would she yield the simple means
She chose to reach the zenith of her art,
When urged by worldlier minds to seek renown,
Nor wait till fame unsought came of itself.

 While now Elizabeth to duties dear
Of home and kindred ties lent all her thoughts,
She sometimes wondered at the flight of time
Since last she held her sister in her arms,
To note with jealous eye if aught of change
Had crept between them or supplanted love,
And youthful purity of deed and thought.
But frequent letters marked the flight of time;
One came from Rome, another Naples, then
Perchance the next from German provinces

Brought greetings filled with cheerful, loving
    phrase.
All climes, all nations that are one with art,
Were each and all made points of pilgrimage.
At last she wrote of Egypt, and was gone
Ere anxious love could pray her stay near home.
And she, devoted now to song, thought not
The world too wide, nor knew that they who wait
Have more of pain than those who do and dare.
Somehow, this voyage brought to mind her first,
And faces rose, with power to move her soul,
And taught that nor toil nor study could
O'ercome the longings of the human heart.
The sunlight as it kissed the wave seemed that
Which filled the day, at sea when listening
To Arnold Deith, he glowingly in words
Had pictured her the Orient—Five years!
How long and yet how swift their flight had been!

And he—had like forgot the "little girl,"
For so he chose to call her then,—one short
And hasty visit as he turned from France
To treat with Mexico for some new code.
A bantering word, a smile half earnest, then
"Good-by," and when she thought him gone, she
    felt
A weight upon her heart which she herself
Could not explain.
        "Good-by," he had returned,
"My sister would God-speed in other guise
Have granted me, since death treats not as guests
The stranger in the land to which I go."
And she, if power of eyes that woo'd her own,
Or glance her sister gave which said, "Be kind,"
Could not have told, but speed of sister then
She gave.
    "God bless you, sir, and bring you safe
To sisters' hearts." And then at thought of them,

More eloquent than words, those orbs fit termed
The soul's reflection, screened themselves behind
A trembling sea of tears, which rested there
As if resolved to wash their color out.
And now, each breeze that blew, the gulls that skimmed
The air, the shadows on the waves, the songs
Of sailors, or the boatswain's call, seemed each
To wake some word he uttered, or his glance.
One day, while dreaming thus, her heart stood still
To see a child that played about the deck
Stand heedless, while a quickly low'ring spar
Was threat'ning death. With cry of fright, she sprang
And seized the fragile babe, that screamed it knew
Not why, as oft contagious fear is worse
Than that we can explain; and Edalaine,
Soothing her fears with tender words and smiles,
Soon found, reclining in her chair, "Mamma,"

Where, helpless, pale, and sad, she sat alone.
Such beauty seldom found a counterpart,
And, as her earnest voice spoke words of thanks,
Its gentle sadness waked in Edalaine
An inward sense that here was one whose need
Of strength to overcome deep-seated woe
Was greater than her own.
      All day she sat
In cheerful converse, or she read, to lead
The thoughts to outward things, nor dared to show
In word or deed the sympathy she felt.
" 'Tis strength she needs," thought Edalaine, made
  wise
By knowledge of the human heart; and so
Each day she ministered unquestioning
A mind disordered by its fears and woes.
" She's stronger than I thought," she said to self,
As day by day she watched the efforts made
To overcome the pressure of some grief

She hid from human eyes, until at length
The child began to droop, and soon they saw
That death stood waiting for the breaking threads.
Within the mother's frame new life infused,
She silently bent o'er her child, to fight
With death, nor spoke, but looked her thanks to all
Who came to aid, or bring new-found relief,
To Edalaine she clung for sympathy,
And oft, when agonized, her eyes made speech
In mute appeal for hope to Edalaine,
It seemed a cruel irony of fate
That one who suffered much must bear yet more.
But come it must, this added grief, and when
One night a murky darkness, blent with roar
Of wind and creak of mast, when waves o'erswept
The vessel's deck, as if to laugh in scorn
At man's presumptuous skill, to send adrift
A mechanism that should dare to cope

With might of stormy winds, the last thread
    snapped
In twain, and life had been extinct for hours
Before they dared reveal the truth to her.
And when it broke upon her sense they stood
Amazed at wildness of her grief.
                            "O wind
And wave, but bear me from this wretched life!
Sole witness of my guilt sustain'd my life.
Chained to my sin, I lived to bear my cross
Until I loved it more than life,—now gone
My punishment is that I live alone!"
In ravings such as these to Edalaine
Somewhat of this poor creature's grief became
Revealed.
        "Poor soul! moer sinned against, I ween,
Then one who sinned. With time alone can grief
Be overcome and peace restored." And so

When strength gave way 'neath such a strain of
    nerve,
To Edalaine and to her maid was left
The friendly care she needed then. Long time
She lay to reason lost, and Edalaine,
Whom sacred trust felt words which came from
    lips
That spoke without the guard of consciousness,
Tried not to heed, till from her lips there fell
A name that made the pulses of her heart
Stand still.

        "O Arnold, Arnold Deith, forgive,
Forgive! nor send me forth to exile worse
Than death!" And then her words, more indistinct,
Became but fitful moan, while she who heard
Sat still as if an icy hand had clutched
Her heart, and held it there relentlessly.
She rose, and faced the night. She tried to think
What fancy turned this blackness o'er her heart.

The heated cabin? Then to chaos turned,
Her thoughts refused to question or reply.
In vain her vision sounded heaven's dark vault,
And naught walked with her there but agony.
Her vow of years ago came back,—"I ne'er
Will wed, e'en though I love. O God, deny
The power to love and all desire!" And now
Was this then love? A maddened jealousy?
A spectre pitiless to haunt her steps
And laugh in wild derision of her woes?
Oh, bitterness to other beings spared!
Why could she not have lived in ignorance
Of heart-aches such as these, and think it grand
To sacrifice a love when most it plead
The worthiness of object loved? But no,
Not so to learn at once she loved, and he
Had another wronged, t' unveil the niche
That held the idol of her heart, and prove

At once its worthlessness, was punishment
She had not thought deserved.

      At last she turned
And sought repose, but still with dumb, white face,
Her eyes oped wide and gazing into space,
She lay all night. "'Tis past," she said at morn.
"I feel no grief, no woe is mine. 'Twas night
That weighted down my heart,—there is no love.
Ah, well, I mean such love as I did dream
Last night." And so, in reasoning, she half
Believed it was a dream, but facing then
The suff'ring stranger, such a pity filled
Her breast, she felt a consecration pure
To ease with loyal sisterhood her grief.
Their voyage ended, still she proffered her
Protecting friendship; paused 'midst cares of art
To minister the balm of hopefulness
Within the lonely heart she felt was pure.
And witnessing the crowned success in song

Of her, so strong and yet so beautiful,
The weaker one oft said, "Your beauty grows,
Dear Edalaine, with loving care you give
Your work. Might I but fill my life with such
A glorious task 'twere yet methinks less sad
To live ; but even voice has been denied
To me, and worthlessly my life drifts on."

    The singer sighed. "Ah, yes, it lightens grief
To work, but you were made to lighten toil
Of others; there alone beside the hearth,
Your work is found." And as the other paled
And shivered, hearing hopeful words like these,
The speaker added, "Yes, I know you think
Them lost for aye ; but mark my promises,—
'Tis better be the person wronged than do
Another wrong."

    "Alas, alas, no more,
I pray, there is no hope for me, no hope!

The very heavens stand appalled at sin
Like mine." And Edalaine, who sought to cheer,
Had made as one is prone, the heart more sad.
"Forgive me, Geraldine," she said, "I wound
Where I would cheer. Let not thy sin do wrong
Beyond itself, but seek for comforting
In higher thoughts. Decide thyself to do
Some good on earth, however sad the heart.
Till grow in courage when the good done man
In daily rounds of ordered tasks revert
At last to cheer thy own poor stricken life."
With spring-time Edalaine had turned toward home,
And that with eagerness. Not all the praise
She took with her could stifle in her heart
A longing for her sister's loving words
And quiet ways. Some chord within her breast
Was out of tune. "'Tis spring," she said, "at home
I'll find with rest a lighter heart," and she

Who'd now become indeed a sister's care
Sobbed out her grief at being left alone.
She dared not say, "Return with me;" she felt
'Twas better not, and so without a word
Of hope, though such she felt within herself,
She said good-by. She had not even heard
Her story, for, when once she strove to speak,
But stopped to struggle with her rising sobs,
Then Edalaine said, "Nay, I can but love
And cherish you for what you are. I know
Whate'er the past, the wrong was not your own
Alone; and suffering that purifies
Has magnified the best that nature gave.
Be hopeful, true unto yourself until
In time you reap both peace and happiness."
And gratefully the little woman twined
Her arms about her generous friend, whose depth
Of generosity she did not dream
(How could she know whom Edalaine had loved?)

She kissed the lips that spoke such confidence,
And watched the steamer westward bound, with eyes
That looked through blinding tears.

        And Edalaine
At home once more, for Paris still she claimed
As home, had found so much of heart-felt love
And peace, she scarce believed her heart e'er knew
A grief. The children that she left were changed
In all but love and confidence, and then
What restful balm she felt her sister's love.

  One day, while wandering slowly through the Louvre,
She met and greeted Arnold Deith. Her words
Playfully spoken, covered up her pain
With seeming raillery and mirth; but how
Her gentle heart beneath it all was pierced
With sorrow, thinking of her Geraldine!
Their friendship was renewed; they wandered oft

Through scenes of art and beauty, and she felt
In wonder at herself a deep belief
That he was innocent of wrong, and then
By duty stifled in her breast, she found
In undercurrents of his words a clew
To base suspicions which devoured her heart
Though sternly holding self responsible
To justice.
        Oft, when softened by the glimpse
Of what in truthful souls would bear the name
Of sentiment, that can be known alone
In souls accord with thoughts sublime, she forced
Herself to find them false as he was base,
Until his very attributes and grace
Of mind appeared arraigned by justice stern,—
The very essence of a villainy
Refined. At other times she shrank with fear
And horror at her own black doubts. "How vile
My mind must be to turn to baser ends

What seems so fair!" and then some whisper soft
Of breezes, bearing on their breath the name
Of Geraldine, gave strength to doubts.

          One eve
They sat beneath the vines till stars came out
Through twilight tremblingly, and night had
  touched,
With soft and solemn melancholy, earth.
The planets whirled above their heads so swift
Their evolutions were not marked, but seemed
To stand in motionless array.

          Of this
They talked when silence fell upon them both.
At last he spoke, as if he gave to thought
Unconscious utterance.

        "What subtle, rare
Delight to sound the soul of one we meet
Unmindful, then, awaking to know our thoughts
Enthralled by mystery that we find in life

Of one but late unknown. You'll ne'er believe
What mystery you are to me, my friend,
I've noted you when least you thought, and much
Have wondered o'er the oneness of your life.
Though gay, you're often sad; though young
    seem old;
Esprit and beauty that would lead not few
To give their lives to pleasure and delight,—
These have no power to lure you from the path
Of meditation, study, and of art.
How few among the narrow world that scorns
The stage could understand all this, when I,
A man that's seen the whole of life, its good
And ill, can scarcely comprehend."
                           And she,
" Why not? Is good so rare, unknown a thing?
The doubting ones find life upon the stage
Impossible with purity; but why?
'Tis true, that 'stead of stern control o'er all

Emotions of the heart, their gifts to bring
Before the world the best and worst of life.
But learn the teachers not themselves as well
The lesson taught?"

    "Alas, such reasoning
Sounds well, dear Edalaine, but see we not
Examples all around of women lost,
Who flaunt their sins upon the stage? And you
Must bear contempt because of them."

      She flushed
A little, then turned pale.

    "That phrase sounds hard;
But some compassion fills my heart for those
Who do not know that while they may contemn
The stage, and find in other fields their means
Of teaching, 'twould be ill of you, who might
Administer some good, where want is known
To say, "Who needs this help must come to me

In place of seeking through the haunts where most
Such needs do congregate.   Upon the stage
We reach a class that come not there for good,
But only seek in life to be amused;
And did we publish it, 'twould likely fright
Them from the door, but all the more must we
Sincerer ones, amidst their pleasure drop
Some seed of good, that all unconsciously
Will spring within their hearts, and then at last
Bear fruit."
    "Ah, yes, but what can one pure girl
Amidst such reckless company e'er hope
To do?   What good from lessons taught by those
The world thinks guilty of immoral deeds?"
A flash of anger sprang into her face,
To his a glimmering smile she did not see.
"You go too far," she said, " for such low minds
Though our contempt out-weight their own, we
  hold

Ourselves above of giving them a thought.

Although 'tis fashion of all ages known

To heap examples of the evils there,

None ever took an equal pains to show

The like in circle of their quiet homes,

Or more (and God forbid they should) within

Their church." And now aroused to keenest sense

Of grief and anger both, the tears rolled down

Her cheeks. "And counted I the wrongs of those

I knew as child and woman, people screened

By influence of home, and those I've known

Since then upon the stage, I'd say at once

Its highway safer far than subtleties

That came to ruin those I left behind.

Oh, could I tell the world what sacrifice

Is hidden 'neath the trappings of the stage!

How nobly struggle timid girls to drive

From door of home its want. I've known poor
    girls
Whose sense of neatness shrank to meet my glance
That boots gave silent witness of their needs,
Or shabby dress was sad and queer exchange
For sheeny costume they had worn but now
Upon the stage. Oh, how my heart has warmed
Toward them, scarce comprehending such a weight
Of life, to know, that, with a sigh that spoke
Content, and yet the piteous thought the sum
Was far too small, the envelope which held
Their pay, unopened, found its way to hand
Of mother, so to pay the needs of home
Which ever seemed to be ahead of toil!"
"But then," he interrupts, "think of yourself;
The most of those you meet have not so fine
A sense of feeling. Think you not that one
Must feel an influence—"

                "I comprehend.

But let us turn to life at home," her tears
Had dried themselves upon the heavy lids
That shrouded eyes whose tenderness seemed half
Appeal through speaking words decisively.
" The man that tends your petted steed, that hands
You forth your whip, the boy who blacks your boots,
The one who trims your hair, or gives by chance
A light for your cigar, who brings the news,—
Are they not of your life essential part?
And yet the abstract portion born to serve.
Their phrases set, you hear each day, your word
Of kindliness, unconsciously bestowed.
They treasure fast within their hearts; but they
Of influence upon your life have none,
And of your day each plays his part, then goes
Forgot till habit calls his services."
" 'Tis not the same," and he, the speaker, shook

His head in doubt, "these people think them-
        selves
Your equal, or your peer, do criticise
Or more, become familiar—that degrades
The most, it does not seem to make you fear."
"Nay, pause," she said, and this time spoke with
        more
Of sternness, which he could not comprehend.
"'Tis said familiar ways breed that contempt
We may full soon resent—ours then the blame.
I understand the scope, you'd say when we
Take in our hands a coal, it leaves upon us there
The token of its black'ning, grimy touch.
Where do we find escape from those whose touch
May bring pollution? In the hearts of men
We own as equals hides there not deceit,
Base treachery, and worse, foul acts against
All justice, mercy, truth, humanity,
Or love?"

"Too true, too true, your words awake
The shadows of a past I dare not now
Disclose," and agitation swept his face
That plainly proved to her his guilt.
"But how
Our words have led us from my first intent,"
He said, when thrice he'd paced the length that lay
Between the garden walls, "for, Edalaine,
My bitter arguments against the stage
Are selfish ones, I love you as **my** life!
And though I've tried full long to stifle love,
Have tried to teach my heart a disbelief
In you, with all the world of womankind,
Your life has cast its radiance round my own,
Has chased away its shadows one by one,
Till once again I look upon the world
To say, 'Some good there yet remains while lives
My Edalaine.' 'Tis strange, you think, to woo
With doubting words, alas, the curse has been

My own. Bring hope, nay heav'n itself renewed
By blessed sounding words that shall bring faith
And drop upon my soul with tender touch
The balm forgetfulness of all that's vile.
For so I think all bitter pain that's dulled
My past would vanish, could I hear thee say
'I love thee, Arnold, and will be thy wife.'"
An icy chill had fallen on the heart
Of Edalaine; she heard the words as if
They were pronounced afar, nor could she think
Or fashion her reply, until he came
And, ere she knew, had clasped her in his arms.
A viper's cold and clammy touch had not
More startled her, she shrank.
      "Nay, Arnold Deith,
Could I but love you, 'twere my least of griefs;
I ne'er should wed, but yet 'twere better live
In loving from afar, than know the God
We worshiped was but clay!"

                        "What problem this?"
He said, "I do not understand."
                            "Thy heart
Its guilt doth better comprehend than words
Of mine.   I know not if with phrase of love,
If promises of future blissfulness
And honor moved the confidence of one
Who, dragged to precipice of wrong, you left,
Without a hope in life. Abhorred of self,
Betrayed by you, she wandered.
                            Well for me
Who shrined an idol all unconsciously
Within my heart, I found her ere too late,
But not too late for her despair, nor my
Poor peace of mind, for ill the heart that aye
Must gaze upon a shattered heap of clay.
Poor Geraldine!"
            He paled. "Poor Geraldine! you met
My wife!" and beads of agony diffused

His brow, and she with wonder-stricken face
Had echoed too, his words of inquiry.
"Your wife? she, Geraldine, is then your wife?"
"She is my wife. She *was* my wife," and when
She would have silenced him, he sternly bade
Her listen. "Stay, for Edalaine, whate'er
Your mandate, I have right to claim respect,
And dare not for my future good leave doubt
In mind of her I love as hope of heaven.
For it *is* my hope of future peace," and pale
As death he faced her whom he dared not touch.
"You think me traitor, doubly so, since I
Have offered love to you. I never thought
My lips could name the past. Indeed, it seemed
To me that if one named its shameful page
Scarce would I hold myself from dealing death
To him who dared to word my deep disgrace."
"Nay, do not tell me," Edalaine had said,
Her only wish the reparation just.

"It must be told, else peace there's none on earth
When you are thinking ill of me. You know
Somewhat my life, that duties in the past
Have often called me from my home,—enough.
My brother is a priest, and when away,
He served as guardian in the home I left.
On one return of absence long, I marked
In person of my wife the signs of guilt—"
And here he faltered, then a moment paused
To gain his strength, and spoke again. "'Twas
    full
Two years before I saw your face. I made
No sign; hence fear was banished, for they knew
I must depart, and so could be deceived.
I watched for guilty paramour of her
Who bore, to thus degrade my honored name.
Oh, shame, oh agony! dissembling thus!
What rage and horror of dishonor felt.
At times I rushed from out the house in fear

Lest passion overcame desire for just
Revenge to strike to earth this woman, who
Had held my name so light. I waited not
In vain, for soon I tracked the pair to this
Same street, and shame, a million times more great
I felt, dishonor, grief, ingratitude
Forced on my soul at once; for he who dealt
The mortal blow was one I'd cherished long.
He was the only one I ever loved
Beyond the parents who had blessed my youth.
But more than that and worse, O Edalaine,
That I must be so cruelly debased,
One mother bore us both!" and here his voice
To whispers that its horror full betrayed
Had sunk.

    "You wonder that I let them pass
With life? I knew their sins would find them out.
I made no sign, but kept them both in view
Till born her child. I faced her with her guilt

And his; but she, with obstinacy strange,
Denied the charge, until I thought her crazed.
I gave her means, and sent her far from home
On pain of utter ruin and disgrace
Before the world. I made him disappear
Unknown to her. The child had reached three
    years
When some one where she dwelt had found a clue
To her identity. Again I sent
Her forth. The child first died, and she in grief
Took ill, was carried from the ship, and then
Came word that, fever setting in, she, too,
Had gone to answer for her grievous sin.
Then came a letter, never read, for why
Take notice of such glaring subterfuge?"
        He paused, and Edalaine—
                "Your reason is
At fault, you quite forget that even sin
Hath right to plead its cause, as you have plead

Unconsciously within my heart by this
Sad tale."

    " O Edalaine, 'tis not the worst!
For five long years, without belief in God
Or man, I've lived to prove that naught remains
But ill; have sought to bring the ruin which
When wrought I spurned with contumely and jest;
Have given curses, and had curses rained
On me."

    His hearer shuddered. "Oh, my friend,
How aches my heart to know that, wronged, you
    know
Not grace of soul to cast its poison forth,
Hast thou ne'er seen the ruddy apples heaped
Upon the ground of some New England field?
Nor marked that when a rotten apple crushed
'Gainst cheek of ruddiest, firmest apple, there
It soon decayed, till, truthfully with you,
One might exclaim, 'They all are rotten-cored,

This apple had a rosy cheek, but see,—
Tis like the rest!' forgetful that its own
Impurity hath brought decay. Good friend,
We make the world, and for our peace of mind
Must shield us from the sin by calling forth
The good. Some gross mistake exists. That you
Were wronged I do not doubt, yet not all wrong.
Your wife who expiates her sin—yes, still
She expiates her sin—start not, your wife
Still lives to suffer; and though woman-born
Myself, and therefore stern disposed, perhaps,
Tow'rd sin that blots th' escutcheon of my sex,
Her grief, her patience, her fortitude, and more,—
Her innocence,—leave me to doubt but that
Her punishment was greater than her sin.
And she more wronged than sinning."

        Arnold Deith
Had buried now his face, his attitude
Was hopelessness itself.

"Oh, Arnold Deith,
Be just, if not for them, your soul's best good
Demands that you should know the very truth."
He started as with anger. "What, debase
Myself by inquiry? What matters it?
The sin was palpable enough. I ask
What palliation of the wrong could there
Exist?"

And Edalaine—"Would not there be
Some comfort, could you know at least the man
You loved had never wronged you; that instead
He sought to guard the honor of your wife,
And you by shielding her? Such things have
    been,
And she"——

"But," angrily he silenced her,—
"Imagination may do much for minds
More weak, but I am right, and that you shield

The acts of those who've wronged me seems most
    strange."
" Nay, Arnold, you do wrong, believe, to my
Best motives; you are hurt and angered, so
At present, cannot understand that souls
Are only ministered by good when free
From that foul taint of sin by others done.
Oh, lay some balm upon thy suffering heart
In thinking though I have been wronged, let me
Be merciful, that mercy may bedew
My life."
    " Ah, Edalaine, 'tis easy said,
But when the iron hath pierced a pride like mine
And at the very moment when I thought
I clutched a saving hand, as once I dreamed
To find in thee, again the ghosts arise
From out the past, to snatch it from my grasp.
Why talk of hope in anything?"
                      " And am

I less your friend than half an hour aback?
Nay, now I feel I *can* be friend, and aid."
"Be friend! I love you, Edalaine, and till
I thought myself quite free to ask your love,
Say, did I not avoid your presence when
It seemed most strange? You never noted it,
But oft I've fled your presence, did not dare
Meet eyes that looked in mine so fearlessly,
Lest they should read the passion of my soul
Awakened by their purity."
      "I knew
I wronged you by my ling'ring doubts. Say more
Than that I cannot, for it is not meet
To broach myself. Recall the words I said
So long ago, 'I ne'er shall wed,' alas,
The sentence hides a life-long woe, which, told,
Might aid your spirit to a nobler trust
In duties of this life above desires.
But that must be when you have proved by acts

The bitterness within your heart has been
O'ercome; and first of all I'd lend in part
Your heart somewhat the pity that I feel
For Geraldine."

    "And would you have me take
Her back again?" his eyes held dangerous light.
" She would not choose to daily read within
Your eyes the guilt upon her soul, if guilt—
A voluntary guilt—there be. But think
You not, in useful life some place would come
If you could meet her once and hear her wrongs?
For such I feel they were."

    "If they were wrongs
Why came she not at once to me?" he said,
Impatient yet at her discourse.

    " Are you
So gentle in your charities that one
So timid did not fear some wrongful act?
And if, I say, once met, you could but say,

'Poor Geraldine, go thou thy way, I'm not
Thy judge, and can forgive what more hath
      wronged
Thyself,' think you it would not bring some peace
Into the desolation of that life?"
" 'Tis very fine, dear Edalaine, but not
The creed that's lettered in my heart, and you
Can scarcely understand (since that you know
Not love) the double bitterness to-day.
Deceived by one, unloved by other, yet
A slave to both. A weaker man would say,
With heartfelt bitterness, 'O Death, where is
Thy sting?'"
      "Ah, that to live needs greater strength
At times than choosing death, all living know.
Nor would we yield with Hamlet that the grave
Hath ills unknown the more than life, for who
Can truthfully foretell the griefs to come?"
And then her own strength feeling much the strain

Of such discourse, she stretched her hand to him.
"Think not, good friend, my life hath not its ills,
Perhaps more hard to bear for being hidden.
Refuse my friendship, mine the loss, nor can
I change the impulse of my heart to hate."
"A woman may, perhaps," he said, "find means
To modify a love to friendship's code.
Not so a man, and I belie my strength
To promise it, at least until I've learned
The magic alchemy you fain would teach,
To touch to sweet the bitterness my life
Hath known. 'Tis pity that the art's not known
More widely." Then with smile of bitterness
Had touched her hand with burning lips, and went
Ere she could frame a last farewell.

         Oh, weight
Of woe! It seemed some dream, and yet her grief
Has mingled with so much of his and that

Of Geraldine, so much of query, hope,
And, too, despair she scarce could tell, if hers
Or theirs, touched most her heart.

BOOK V.

And now a cloud had settled over France
Had crept above the brilliant capitol,
Until its slowly gathering folds had wrapped
Themselves about its spires, crept through its
    streets,
Enveloping and clouding all its cheer,
And ominous, was heard at intervals
The sound of musketry. "Our youth do fear
To lose their skill," some said, but wiser ones
Then shook the head and murmured, "Nay, not so,
Such sounds portend much graver mark; and balls,
Not shot alone do there resound, and spurt
Of blood responds to well timed aim. The air

Is foul with presence of an enemy."
And then again the sounds had ceased, to be
Forgotten, timid ones took heart, these last,
The maid that waited for her bridal morn,
Or mother of some noble son who burned
To walk in footsteps of his fallen sire.
And oft this last, from out some sacred nook,
Or recess of their humble homes, took down
The gun tow'rd which from earliest youth he'd
    looked
With vague alarm, and then, when older grown,
Had listened to its history with cheeks
Aflame, resolved if ever war broke forth,
That gun should bring him victory, or death.
And now, in secret, lest the wish out-sped
The coming of the storm, with loving hand,
The youth, while fancy painted pageantry
Of war where prancing steeds and cries, "*La France
Et Liberté aussi,*" brought victory,

He polishes the sturdy steel, half awed
To think his sire one time had done the same.
"But now we meet another foe, *ma foi!*'
He mused, "*les gens là!* to think to conquer us!"
And not too soon, each peasant grasped his gun.
The cloud descended till it wrapped their loved,
And beauteous city in its treach'rous folds,
And strangers, whether pleased or not, could find
No means to make escape. Some felt to flee
Was sheer ingratitude tow'rd nation that
Had sheltered them in prosperous days, and made
The cause their own. Dean Brent was one of these,
And Edalaine had said, "I too can aid."
Her sister feared for her. "Is't not enough
My husband gives his skill and we our work
At home?" But Edalaine saw greater need
Within the teeming hospitals. "Not all,"
She said, " had teaching such as we at home,

Nor know the skillful touch these sufferers
Do need." And so there burned upon her breast
The Scarlet Cross; that sacred sign that made
Of foes a brotherhood. Where'er she walked
Its gleam oped wide the ranks to let her pass.
Confusion's self, would oft give way at sign
Or word, "I am a servant of the cross."
One day they came to say a lady ask'd
For her, and through the crowded wards she walked,
Too full of homely cares to wonder or
To ask "What name?" At cry half plaintive, half
Afraid, of "Edalaine!" she clasped with joy
The trembling form of Arnold's wife. "You are
Not angry that I came, 'twas you advised
To choose some useful work, and I am come
To do somewhat my share."

"But you, so frail,—"
Cried Edalaine, then seeing tears begin

To rise within the limpid eyes, lest come
She prove unwelcome, " here in truth you'll find
The need of gentle hand and tender look,
They often soothe severest wound beyond
The doctor's skill."
    And Geraldine soon felt
Her usefulness, forgot herself amidst
The suffering, until a dainty pink
Shone through the lilies of her face, and light
Of happiness had brighten'd sombre eyes.
A faithful bearer of the cross, content
She ne'er had known now dwelt within her heart.
The name of Arnold Deith ne'er passed the lips
Of Edalaine, who mused, " Why probe a wound
Till healing can be brought, and now sometimes
She feared it never could be done, she saw
As yet no clear solution of the way
To straighten, in the embittered lives of those
She fondly loved, such strangely tangled threads.

At times she tried to doubt of Geraldine.
Impossible! And once she questioned her.
"Dear Edalaine, my brain has near gone mad
In efforts vain to solve the mystery
That shrouds the sin that blots my life. The sin
'Tis like you have divined, but more than that,
I would I might relate, an endless round
Of queries in my mind o'er problem that
Is never near solution, frights a mind
More strong than mine, and Oh, dear Edalaine,
Your confidence and love have brought me hope
That gives me strength to live!"
       'Midst roll of drum,
The call of troops, excitements, fears and ills
Of the besieged and anxious city, thoughts
Found daily cares that crowded from the mind
One's individual woes. Sometimes a word
From Arnold Deith reached Edalaine. He too
Had found much need of work. To Edalaine

He wrote to flee the dangers yet unknown;
Still found it in his power to aid her leave
The now beleaguered city, would she go?
"You are unkind," she answered him, "to wish
Me comprehend that only helplessness
Can be the lot of womankind. Men stay,
And why not I, since envious the work
They do, urged on by roll of drum, the sound
Of thrilling strains, till these are merged to din
And roar of battle, clash of steel, and cries
That fire ambitious souls to something outside
The consciousness of personal alarms.
Our countrymen would say: how strange that you
And I, nay, all Americans that fired
To deep enthusiasm, do their part.
'Tis not their land, it's hardly natural!
Has then humanity a native land?
And too, what happiness the thought, whoe'er
The exile, quick to sympathize and do,

But may not find a welcome in the hearts
Of suffering humanity.   To-day
A soldier died upon my arm.   His one
Faint smile, the last, would aid me toil for those
Who are not learned in gentle gratitude.
Our best in this strange labyrinth,—the right
And wrong of life, is done because we say
We knew not how to help ourselves.   And then
Some kindly soul would flatter us.   We are
Inspired now the word recalls the fact
You told me once I was inspired and must
Succeed.   May not one be a second time
Inspired, this time to drop awhile the thought
Of selfish aims?" And so the letter closed.
Yet Edalaine had been unlike her sex
Had not such thoughtful care brought restfulness,,
And with it feelings of security.
Steadily disease amidst the maimed

Crept in, and touched the brow of one, breathed
    o'er
The lips of others till, unwelcome guest,
He held the secrets, ruled with dread the house.
Fearlessly amidst contagious ills
And added cares, walked Edalaine, her calm
And cheerful spirit lending hope to those
Who would have fled from out the wretched place.
Nor was the dread procession at an end.
The weighty ambulance—forerunner grim
Of blight, disease, of pain and death itself,
Came day or night to leave its moaning charge.
One day, as Geraldine had loosed the band
That half concealed the face of one poor man,
Who, conscious, suffered agonies of death,
She gave a cry, and, ere they reached her side,
Fell fainting to the floor.
                      "Poor child," they said,
"The sight was more than she could bear."

"Alas!"
The doctor sighed, "I fear 'tis more than fright.
She has been brave enough ere now, at sight
Of cruel marks of hatred and of strife,
May God forbid it being fell disease."
When Edalaine had seen her friend restored
To speech, she said:
    "No more to-day, my friend
You must have rest."
    "Oh, no, it was not that—
I thought, O grief!"—and then her lips turned
  pale,
And once again she slipped from consciousness.
'Twas long before her eyelids oped themselves,
And then the doctor would not let her speak.
"Be quiet, dear," entreated Edalaine,
"Myself will take the cares that fall to you."
A grateful glance scarce answered her, ere gone.
She understood, when bending o'er the cot

Of him the surgeons sought to ease, and felt
Her own heart give a sudden bound of fright.
" How foolish, yet there is a likeness found.
Poor child, I understand ! How well she hides
The grief that's ever present to her heart !'
'Twas midnight. Long the patient slept through aid
Of drugs the doctors left, when suddenly
He spoke : " Ah, look, 'tis he ! My brother leads
The column on the right, I'll reach his side
Or meet my death ! Say, friend, remember this,
If fate decrees that I must fail, you'll find
The papers here, which give into his hand,—
Oh, God ! I'm lost—they're ordered to the rear !
The foe now moves between my friends and me !
I see him now,—alas ! he falls,—if death,
I'd scarcely yield a sigh, so welcome like
Would be to me ! Thank God, 'tis come, I die !"
At this he sprang upright, when Edalaine

Till now a startled listener, had touched
His arm.
      "Be quiet, sir, you're safe with friends,
Your papers lie beside your hand.   All's done
That can be done till health returns to you."
Amazed, he gazed upon her face.
      "Till health—
I thought the end had come, and must I die again?
Who knows? I may be doomed, alas,
To hundred deaths?"
      "Not so, good friend, the death
We most do fear more lenient is, perhaps,
Than Pain, who sometimes takes upon himself
His semblance pale."
      Soothed once again by words
Of hopefulness, the patient slept for hours.
When next he woke, long time he lay in thought,
Or watched the face of Edalaine that now,
Deep lost in meditation, witness bore

Of ever present grief.　At last aware
He wakeful lay, she bent above the cot.
"You're better, sir, can aught be done for you?"
"I'm better, yes, the calm preceding death.
My pain is gone, affrighted by the touch
And chill of death that's creeping through my
  limbs.
Nay,—listen, 'tis but truth: Sometimes the vail
Is torn from off our sight, revealing sense
Of things unknown in health, so now with me.
Thine eyes beseech me live for sake of friends,
They also tell me trust my woes to thee.
Then lend me now thy listening ear to learn
A tale that proves our very virtues are,
Sometimes, the pitfall of unwary feet.
We claim we have the will to make our world
When circumstance can weave intangibly
A chain, to trip the footsteps of the wise,
That once unlinked would make him seem a fool.

In youth I came to France. My father's wealth
Placed all advantages of knowledge 'neath
My very hand, and more than that, I spent,
As boys will do, a goodly share of time
In folly and in search of pleasures vain.
It fell that, in a home to which my name
Had given free access, I met a girl
Whose beauty woke my youthful heart to love.
Both loved—but vainly. All my wealth could not
Atone for differences of birth, lest that
She followed me to share my native land.
The more they sought to break the bond, the more
We clung to love, until our fate was sealed.
We planned a flight, but were betrayed and failed,
And she was sent from Paris to the home
Of one who nursed her as a child. But love
Finds means to balk his enemies, and gold
Unlocks the strongest bars. I found her nurse.—
Enough. At last in secret we were wed.

The months rolled by, a child was born, and still
Her parents thought her banishment but just,
And righteous chastisement in that she e'er
Declared herself not yet content to yield.
Alas! though safely passed a period
We feared might bring discovery, there came
A sudden call for me to turn tow'rd home.
My father ill, I dared not find excuse,
And, torn between two terrible extremes,
I said farewell; but she, as if her strength
Refused one grief the more, had breathed her last,
'Ere I had reached my home, while till the last
She prayed her parents ne'er should know the truth.
'Tis useless that I here repeat the grief,
Despair and hopelessness my life then knew,
And had our child not lived, my strength to face
My life had fled with hers.
     At last I hid

My heavy grief beneath the garb of priest,
And so estranged my father's heart.   One friend,
My brother, now remained to me, and he
Upheld my steps through days of poverty
And grief, nor knew what drove me thus to wear
The heavy cross.   At last he too, was wed.
There is no love,' he said, ' on either side,
It is my father's wish, through pride of birth.
She weds me for my father's gold, I—well,
I have not loved and am not like to know
Its mastery—why should I not please him?
His bitterness against one son is quite
Enough.'

   I shuddered at his coldness then,
For, many years my junior, yet he seemed
A cynic born.

   His wife was young and gay,
But pure and amiable, nor seemed to know
How serious 'twas to wed, and, from the first,

I vowed, scarce thinking that such oath could
    mean
So much, to guard from her all ills that might
Beset her path, and wake to grief the man
I loved above all else.
                One day she came
For absolution—for her faith was mine—
'O holy father, absolution make
For sins of thought; a youth has come
Into my life, and though we never spoke,
His ardent gaze hath taught me life hath much
I cannot understand,—I scarce can breathe
When looks he so, and 't seems to me I do
His will and not mine own.'
                      I questioned her,
I gave advice, and more, I followed her
To see with mine own eyes the youth who thus
Had waked a sleeping heart. Alas, alas!
Oh, complications strange of daily life!

It was my son! and yet not claimed as mine.
He knew me only as his teacher, friend,
And confidant. I turned tow'rd home half stunned.
My brother absent oft for months, knew not
The peril of unloved, unloving wife.
And I scarce knew how best to interfere
Without some serious harm. And day by day
I waited. Sad mistake! The torrents vast
Of pent-up love are swifter, fiercer far
Than else can be." The speaker paused to breathe
And tried to speak again, " And Geraldine "—
But here his voice had fluttered on his lips,
A purplish, ghastly white shot o'er his face,
The light within his sunken eyes was quenched,
And Edalaine, in sudden agony,
Hung o'er the senseless form to know if this
Indeed were death. It could not, must not be,

That death would place his seal upon a truth
Important to her heart! the brother this,
And had he not desired to tell the tale
To clear himself?

     At last a flicker touched
His lips, 'twas scarce a breath, but like a shade
That touches trees and flowers so light we half
Believe it fancy of our sight, for clouds
Are absent from the sky, it touched his cheek,
Then moved across his brow and o'er his lids
Had trembled. Once again she touched his lips
With cordials, rubbed emaciated hands, and
Stroked the pallid brow until the lids
Had slowly lifted, but the poor, weak lips
Could frame no words. Once more she bathed the
  lips.
"Too late, read this!" the lips then whispered her,
"I did my best, my best, forgive, for—!"
She closed the eyes and gently loosed the hands

That grasped against his breast the written word,
Laid straight the limbs, then closed the sightless
    eyes,
And all within the room, scarce consciously,
Placed carefully to rights.
                    "Poor soul! too late to reach
The goal forgiveness, yet I feel his life
Was marked by some great act of sacrifice.
Be mine the happiness," she mused, "to swift
Completion crown the work he left undone!"

   *   *   *   *   *   *   *   *

As morning broke upon the slumbering world
In presence of the dead, with reverent hands
She slipped the ribbon from the written sheets
And read:
                "Oh, punishment, more fleet thy course
To overtake unwary, stumbling feet!
My cross was weighty ever, now, alas,
I sink beneath its added grief and care!

One day while I absorbed in study sat
Alone, my son, for so I dare to call
Him here, burst, unannounced, upon the room.
His face was pale, his manner wild, distracted.
Beholding me, he wrung his hands and cried:
'Oh, holy father, pity me and take
My life! I cannot, dare not live! My look,
My touch pollutes this holy place, pollutes
Your presence! Pity me, and take my life!'
Long time it was, while agony my heart
Had filled with dire imaginings of wrong,
Ere I could learn from him the crime he wept.
Oh, shame! I scarce can pen the wretched tale!
He long had followed Geraldine, and felt
Himself at first by her beloved, and then
She would not meet his pleading eyes, or glanc'd
But coldly at him when he passed. He swore
Some enemy had poisoned her against
His love, as if she knew his friends or foes!

And then, Hope bearing him on wide-spread
    wings,
He vowed such love as his could only live
As echo of her purer heart. 'She loves,
As I love her, could I but reach her side!'
And more and more his love to madness burned,
When, following that day, he found
The maid had left her seated in the ' Bois'
Alone, and watching there her lovely face,
He saw her head droop 'gainst a tree until
She slept.
        'My love!' he whispered bending there,
'What chance but fate that leaves thee to my care?'
And as he gazed, temptation seized and ruled
The fevered spirit of his heart. Within
His breast he bore an Oriental drug,
Most potent 'gainst all evils and disease ;
Or drawn into the lungs the dreamy soul

Could steep in ecstacy, or warp the will
To stronger minds. Swift glancing round that
 none
Observed, he placed upon her dainty lace
A crystal drop from which arose like mist
A subtle odor,—first a tremor moved
Her blue-veined lids, and then her lips apart
Like leaves of roses trembled to a smile.
An instant served to bear her from the spot
To hail a carriage and be gone. And here
The youth with sobs was shook, then spake:

'Oh, joy
Supreme, to bear her in my arms, my life,
My own! And frenzied quite with joy, I reached
My street, dismissed the man, and hastened thro'
The court, as yet observed by none. I clasped
My treasure! How I joyed o'er her, and when
The drug was nearly spent, her senses scarce
Beneath the spell, what new delight to feel

Her conscious that caresses showered themselves
On her, until a dagger pierced my heart,
When, in her murmured words I heard her name
Another! "Husband, then you love your wife!
And 'tis no shame to feel my pulse beat high
With love for thee!" At words like these my heart
Stood still, the rapture of its purer love
Then died, and hate for him, desire for her
Alone remained—and, holy father, there
The innocent doth lie, of crime I've done,
Unhappy victim! while I know too late
As, waking to its dread enormity,
I've only earned her hatred and contempt.'
'She waked to consciousness?' I sternly asked.
'To consciousness, and yet she never ceased
To name me Arnold, and her love.'
      'Thank God
For that!' Forgetting then my priesthood's
 vows,

My love for him, with curse I drove him forth.
A father's awful curse, and threatened him
With instant death, if e'er he ventured near
The shores of France.

     I saved my brother's wife
From lightest word, for she awoke at home.
Ofttimes she wore a strange and puzzled air,
Or oped her lips as if she'd speak to me,
Then hesitation turned her speech. One day,
Confessing sin that she had feared, not done,
She said: 'I cannot tell,—but memory
Or dreams do mock my thoughts,—my husband
  came,
And Oh, my father, love was born in me,
A love I never knew before, and then
A blank came o'er my dream, and now I know
'Twas vain, although my consciousness cannot
Gainsay its truth.'

Some months had passed when you,
My brother, came, and oft I trembled lest
You saw the change.

'My dreams were mockery,'
She said to me, ' My husband seems more stern
Than e'er before, and when I told my dream
He gazed at me with bitter scorn! His looks
Demanded secrets which I ne'er have held.'
Alarmed at this, I bore for her a guilt
Of which her soul was pure. Her health declined,
And more the puzzled air dwelt on her face.
I then persuaded her a doctor seek,
And he in turn, through sign from me, had pressed
Upon her mind the needs of country air.
Aware of what now menaced her, I firm
Resolved to hold from you the wretched truth,
The consequence of other's sin.

You traced
Our steps, and laid the blame of wrong on me.

Too deeply stunned, I dared not tell the truth,
I dared not rouse within her mind again
The image of the youth whose glance had waked
Her heart, then left it guarded by its own
Fair innocence. I could not then betray
My son, and silently I bowed to blame,
Too late aware it was my greatest sin.
God knows 'twas much to give in love for thee;
For her, and him, the son I cursed and loved.
That day thy rage had torn me from the spot,
Yet all my thought was grief for Geraldine,
Who stood accused of guilt unarmed with proofs
Of innocence.
   Three years I passed on seas
Of trackless breadth before I found the means
To turn toward home, and when I came I found
No trace of her. I entered the defence
Of Paris, there at least I found a clue
I thought would lead to thee. I could not die,

And hope to sleep in peace, with weight of wrongs
Like these upon my soul. Alas, I fail.
The changing scenes, the perils of these times
Do mock me all, God grant my strength fail not."
And here the story ended, while his pen
Had added, with a trembling hand, the words:
"In that I loved thee much, my best beloved,
My brother, suffered I the more. Alas!
It hath not spared to thee a bitter grief.
How can we mortals choose the way? Our best
Is oft the worst, and he who tangles first
The tiny threads that weave the mesh of life,
Is tripped thereby his weary life-time through!
Forgive, my brother, Geraldine, forgive,
And love at least thy brother's memory,
Who'd gladly give his worthless life for thee
And thine." And then bedewed with many a tear,
Was traced the boyhood's name, and Edalaine,

With swelling heart exclaimed, "God grant to him
His written prayer!"

* * * * * * *

Not at an end the cares of Edalaine.
The dead to earth restored, her living charge
Was Geraldine, whose fluctuations 'twixt
The grave and life, had filled her anxious heart
With sad misgivings.

    Geraldine had said:
"The end is come, why seek to baffle death?
The summer ends with winter blasts; the leaves,
When nature fills requirements of her law,
Do fall to mingle with the earth again.
I do not ask why was I born, who knows?
The butterfly that flutters through one day
Has like, less need to ask," and Edalaine—
"Hush, child, the moths devote to tasks of love
Tow'rd fellow creatures, must have taught thee laws
Of recompense. Look back upon your youth

That now seems distant, less from years than pain.
Had joy the conscious meaning of to-day?
"The meaning of all earthly joy is past.
To thrilling of one word life's pulses stir,
And that would prove, I think, the golden key
To open wide the doors of future bliss.
Forgiveness mine, my pilgrimage is done.
Nay, Edalaine, chide not the wish to die.
'Tis God that taketh thus the sting of death,
By dimming worldly joys when comes the hour
To go—this peaceful longing to be gone,—
The blessing from His hand, disarming death.
The sweetest joys of life would seem a weight
I could not choose, and if I long to hear
One voice again, 'tis that I know while sweet
To be forgiven, so forgiving brings
Its blessedness, and I my saddened life
Would end with twice-told blessings crowned."

                                    And she,
The listener, was silent. "Will he come?"
"You know, dear Edalaine," the other spoke,
" I never loved the man I wed and wronged,
Until too late. I was a child to whom
They pictured life of freedom; sacrificed
My youth to spare the name my father bore.
I ne'er had learned as yet what freedom meant.
And when I might have learned, 'twas there I
    failed!
Oh, Edalaine! What have I done to bring
Upon my life and those who claimed respect,
Such shame?" And like a wounded deer, her
    eyes
Bespoke her agony, then drowned themselves
In tears whose passion frightened Edalaine.
    Her plaint, the only witness of her grief,
Seemed come from out a tortured heart that half

Was frightened when 'twas done, that she had
   dared
Complain, though suddenly it swept across
Her weary heart the wrong she had endured.
" Be calm, dear Geraldine, I pray, such grief
Endangers life, I could not tell it you
Before, you were too ill, and now I wish
You were content with sole assurance that
The accusation 'gainst your name must be
Withdrawn, by proofs that echo from beyond
The grave. There is no conscious wrong for which
To plead forgiveness." So at last she soothed
The stricken one.
                    At midnight came a sound
Of clattering hoofs, and softly Edalaine
Had led the way to bed-side of her friend.
" There's some one here, dear Geraldine."
                                   " I know,"
She said, " I heard the horseman, then the step

Of Arnold. God hath marked the sparrow's fall,
I die in peace if he—"
                      And Arnold clasped
Her in his arms.
                "Poor, suffering dove!
What sacrifice would not be made if all
That's past could be undone. Poor Geraldine!
Forgiveness from your lips were sweet. To ask
I dare not." Edalaine then softly closed
The door upon a scene she thought to see
Was worth the being born.
                    When later she
Returned, the dawn was resting o'er the land;
Already had it drawn in clear-cut lines
Each branch or vine that clambered o'er the Church
That served them in this time of need as house
Of refuge for the sick, and as the wind
Had swayed religiously the trees, it seemed
To Edalaine that Peace then moved across

The scene to leave a benediction o'er
The sleeping world.
     Like chiseled marble lay
The lovely face of Geraldine against
Her husband's breast, but when he spoke, she oped
Her eyes and smiled on Edalaine.
        "Good-bye."
And then he stooped to catch her murmured words.
"Remember—love, my—Edalaine—dear Ar—!"
The weary life was done.

  *   *   *   *   *   *   *   *

      The longed-for peace
Had come to France, and while the scars of strife
Must live for generations in the hearts
Of men, time covered o'er its ruder touch
On wall, on temple; tower, of war-swept towns,
And once again fair Paris ruled the world

Of fashion ; once again awoke to art,
And lured its students from all lands and climes.
The life of Edalaine, since fearlessly
She bade a last farewell to Arnold Deith,
Had lost its charm—'twas when he told to her
The dying words of Geraldine and said:
"The angel choir must weep if we do part."
"'Twere better that their tears bedew the right
We do, than weep a curse I'd bring mankind."
And then she told him what her cross must be.
" Oh, Edalaine, thou art too sensible,
To let the chatter of those ignorant
Old dames such gloomy heritage portend
To wrong thy strong young life and wreck my love.
And if thy fear and reasoning were just,
Who has more right to dedicate their life
To thee, what'er it bring?"

"Thou, Arnold Deith,
Wouldst make such sacrifice, wouldst choose a
    wife
Whose light may go out utterly, not pale
To silence while the senses fail; their last,
Best sense, the seeing, hearing, touching thee?
Not that, but go out horribly, one sense
Betraying all the rest. Mine eyes see hate
Within thine eyes; this life discolored, till
The strangeness of my glance would sting thee
    more
Than venom of a serpent, telling thee
It is thy love's—thy wife's, or if escaped—
(And here, like rose that sleeps within a shell,
The color dyed the rounded cheek, then swept
Off white the coral lips) and if escaped
(I have escaped as yet) a score of years,
How could you bear our children weighing words
Of her—their mother, glances sharp as prick

Of needles shoved straight to the eye, not less
The sure that furtively it's done?"
                              " Nay, love,"
" Nay, Arnold, perfect love like thine was meant
For no such sacrifice in saying yes,
As woman's lonely heart would lead me do,
For building me a niche above the needs
Of love, my weary wings oft flutter prone to earth
Of other women, till my reason cries
Who, what art thou, that seekst to float an isle,
And live without the distance man proscribed
Of air, nor breathe like them the oxygen allowed,
And when thy lungs hath used its store, flat falls
Thy weight as theirs might do.   In saying yes,
This yes of other women, easy said,
I'd feel a doom pronounced to happiness
That now lives sole in knowledge of this love,
That is so great it deems no sacrifice,
To still declare in face of witnesses

Like these, my life long fears,—I love thee, love,
My Edalaine, and live to wear thee on
My breast."
          The words like burning lava poured
Across her lips that seemed, with all her form,
A carven image cold to look upon.
And once she smiled—why, tears were not so sad,
And she who never spoke that all her form
Was not in consonance and thrilled to tips
Of rosy fingers, she, whose earnest soul
Was animate in every graceful curve
Of neck, of wrist, of silence' self, now stood
A frozen image of herself, and spoke
As if she feared to hear her own sad words.
And he who listened was not, strange to tell,
Quite dumb to understanding of her strange
And frozen way, and then, as if to melt
The ice with which she proudly clothed herself,
He caught her in his arms and wept o'er her,

With sudden kisses wiping out each tear
That fell from his upon her drooping face.
Releasing gently hands that held her fast,
She looked at him again.

"No hope?" Alas,
The gloom remained within her eyes, and there
He read his doom, and so once more he went
'Midst dangers, while she turned to walk alone.
But art had lost its power, or else she found
Her labors there too far from definite
Fruition of their useful ends, and so,
Oft questioned with herself, if life were not
Unhinged, or else quite narrowed to the aim
Existence only, then confessed to self—
A woman, not an angel, mind—confessed
Discouragement that art in song—the song
That reached perfection, found no wider scope
For mind, then technical precision, like
Some mechanism which, once set, will make

Its ceaseless round.   A wheel within a wheel
Will do the same, or engine at the touch
Of master hand will speed the iron horse.
And yet when borne upon the soaring wings
Of soul-inspiring verse and perfect sound,
These leaden weights, reality, were lost,
And only sense of freedom—love, what love
Should be, enthralled her being then, until
Intoxicated with its pain or joy,
She'd cry: "How blesséd is the power of song!"
But oftener of late she felt constrained
To muse: "'Tis art alone I give the world,
For well I know the difference.   My song
Has lost its soul," and then, half smilingly,
"It sure has gone a-gypsying," the smile
Then dying to a sigh, she thought on one
Who urged her once to sing, and, since he went,
She'd rather weep.

What weather vanes we are,
We women, fit to do, we think, what men
Have done, and then a passing face sets nerves
A-tremble, till our awkward hand has blurred
The figures on the black-board of our lives,
And, all at once, the problem (nearly solved
We thought) has lost its interest. We'd rub
It wholly out but that we'd shame our past
Perverseness. Now we wish, without the need
Of knowing 'tis a wish, that he might come,
And, holding fast resisting hands (we still
Resist,) would take the sponge and deftly blot
It out and set *his* problems there, or else
Solve ours for us with flattering words, "You soil
Those gentle hands, I see you have it, leave
To me the finishing, while you look on."
And then, safe sheltered in his arms, what ease
To see mistakes and point them out, till he
Thinks woman's wit beyond his own.

One night
She stood before a listening throng that drank
The music that her lips poured forth, as if
Athirst for all she gave. With every note
They longed for more, when all at once a cry
Rang through the place, that sent a thrill of fear
And horror to each trembling heart.
"Dear friends,"
The singer spoke, and something in her look
Made each one pause to listen.
"I am 'twixt
The fire and you. I then beseech you, one
And all, take no alarm, while here I wait
Your quiet exit, life depends on that."
And then, as if her will held back the ones
Who felt themselves hemmed in by surging crowds,
The tide swept slowly out, their latest glance
Tow'rd her who stood like gleaming angel that
Had said, "Obey, and I will give you life."

Till last the waiting ones who watched her face,
Thereon to read its hope or fear, were free
To go, when some cried out to her in fear,
As now they saw the darting flames above
Her head, or dropping brands of fire. And one
Rushed back to seize her bodily. But no,
Before the stage was reached, she moved aside.
The lines that held the curtain burned away,
It fell with stunning crash between the two,
A sheet of angry flame. The stranger paused
To feel an iron hand upon his arm.
"Go, seek your friends, 'tis mine the task to save
Or perish there with her!" And then the smoke
Swept through the place and hid the face of him
Who spoke, to disappear amidst the flames.
The fierce, mad element licked out each mark
Of art within the place, devoured the walls
With wild insatiate hate, and filled the hearts
Of those that watched, with awe and thankfulness

At their escape, or agony of fear
For those who not yet found might be amidst
The flames. And when a cry of joy had sped
From lip to lip, they knew that Edalaine
Had been from peril freed, unconscious yet
To what had passed or loving words of him
Who imperiled life in saving her.

        The morn
That marked the horror of the night with charr'd*
Remains, revealed that five poor victims lay
Beneath the ruined walls, and Edalaine
The sacred duty took upon herself
To give them kindly burial, and wept
Above the blackened forms of those who were
Her humble aids while striving so to reach
True excellence.

---

 * Five pupils of Francesco Lamperti were burned in an Opera House at Nice, and Julia Valda, an American then singing there, took charge of the remains. The mæstro was unable to continue his duties for a year, such was the shock to his nerves.—AUTHOR.

One day when all was past,
And wonderingly she mused upon her own
Escape, and marveled that she ne'er could learn
The name of him who saved her life that night,
The servant entered, bringing her a card.
"Dear Edalaine," it read, "I scarce dare come,
But something tells me that misfortune claims,
As ever, gentle treatment at your hands,
And I have such a longing for the voice
Of some old friend, I cannot wait the day
My ills have passed from me." And she with heart
Whose strong emotion choked her voice, had said:
"Please send to me the bearer of this card."
Then looked as if she fain would flee the room.
And when a moment later, pale but calm,
The face of Arnold Deith,—the broad, white brow
The full and speaking eyes, had met her own,
She stood a palpitating presence, while
The well-known music of his voice had said,

In playful tone, the speech pathetic made
By truthfulness:
   "You see we stand apart.
You needs must come to me, for though I still
Can clasp your hands in two strong, friendly ones,
I cannot reach your side quite yet without
This aid." And here he marked with glance a
   crutch.
She did not move, but seemed denied the power.
Then, o'er her face there grew a glowing light,
As, struggling with a doubt, it breaks away.
The light transfused her eyes and speaking face,
And with its glory she had seemed transformed.
A mantle that had wrapped her round, seemed
   then
To fall away,—the darkness of the doubt,
And radiantly, as if she trod on air
Or borne along by his desire, she reached
His outstretched waiting arms, for o'er *his* soul

The light had shed its glory, bringing joy
He thought had been unborn for him. All earth
Had turned to chaos as these two did solve
The problem in a kiss, whose lingering touch
Of passion breathed a sigh whose rapture swelled
The chord of ecstacy to break against
The shores of infinite bliss in shuddering moan.
And she at last had voiced : " I might have known
Who came to save a life I held but light
If sacrificed for full a thousand lives !"
And he with happy eyes: " Just that, I claimed
What you had thrown away as valueless.
You see," he laughed, " my generosity
Was born of earth and is perhaps at fault.
The life once yours is mine to hold and keep,
I would not, if you wished, restore it you."
At which, though silently, she looked at him,
Her tender smile was tremulous with tears.
The twilight sank to dusk, the dark to night,

And still their thoughts were linked in ready
  words,
The leaves of roses pricked together each
With tiny thorn, as children weave in play
Their garlands. So they made, more gravely,
  shroud
To twine about the past at burial.
And some without the thorns were garlanded,
To strew, with eager heart, the path that stretched
Beyond their feet. So strange that emblems serve
So differently. We weep for grief, and yet
How easy 'tis to show'r our joys with tears.
A lark shot upward, caught the growing light
Upon the wing, and sent to sleeping earth
Ecstatic notes that herald joyous morn.
The house cat stretched upon the narrow edge
Of latticed fence, oped wide her green-gray eyes,
To bathe them with the lambent light, and touch
To yellow gold their sleepy disks, then stretched
Her suppleness to lazier comfort. Leaves,

Dyed black by night, assumed their dainty green,
And then a flame of red shot o'er the sea
Before he rose and whispered:

     "Edalaine,
My pilgrimage is like the conqueror
Who went from home in humble guise, but who
Returning wears the royal crown and robes.
'Tis more than I deserved, or hoped of late."
"Ah, hush!" she said, "the conqueror must still
Be merciful in dealing with the conquered,
Or like worthy diplomat, receive a gift
As if the favor were conferred else that
My wilfulness betray again my heart.
Your pow'r has waked me from the night-mare
  fear,
And lo! at your command, 'Believe,' I place
My fingers wonderingly within the wound
That's left by cruel nails upon the cross,
And confident reply, 'I do believe.'
And generous, you promise me my art—

Though man, in thinking it a bauble toy.
But I accept the gift as if you knew
Its worth.   I willingly o'erlook the slight
In recognition of the sacrifice,
It may, perchance (though but a toy), demand.
I know at last the loneliness of fame,
The incompleteness of a life when once
The magic hand has swept its slumbering strings
To sound of love.   I now can sing as ne'er
Before.   My life divided 'twixt my art
And thee, had lost its power.   Once more I know
Completion, and can verify the truth.
How slow we are to grow in mind!   I thought
My art had nothing more, because my life
Stood still.   But art is broader, higher yet
Than fame.   To stop at fame were robbing art
Of highest worth, the inner consciousness
Of what art is, not comprehended quite
By those who dip our name in crucible
That luminous, is moulded to the word

Of 'Fame.'
    And he, with slowly budding smile:
"But what will say the world of him who lets
The bird once caged, wing other flights?"
         "Ah, there
We meet again the blindness that hath naught
Of sight beyond the meagreness of fame.
One says, 'I'd never let my wife take wing.'
Confessing so, and unaware, the man's
Pure selfishness. That man would let his wife
Bake bread, or mend his vest, go fetch his boots,
His slippers, cap, his coat or wine; do all
Those things a servant better might have done,
Learned only in such usefulness of life,
And thinks himself unselfish that he takes
From out her hand life's chosen work. He clips
Her ready wings, until, no matter what
Her flutterings may be, she fain must stay
Content to hop around the homestead hearth,
To peck the crumbs there thrown to her, and ape

Humility that's born without the wings."
He smiles indulgently, to hear her talk
Half bitterly, and half with that contempt
That's born observing yet the serfdom laid
On womanhood, and whispered:
                        "What of her
Whose noble strength has stemmed the storms?
    Will she
At last be glad to fold awhile the wings;
Those weary wings, and rest at home with me?"
"How, traitor, born a diplomat, I need
Not say, be diplomatic still, you'd have
Your way, convincing me I have my own!"
"Oh, sweetest lips that ever spoke a truth,
You steal my very thoughts and so I seal,
The future while your lips are formed to shape
The dear impertinence,—'Can love e'er tell
What love may do?'"

FINIS.

www.ingramcontent.com/pod-product-compliance
Lightning Source LLC
Chambersburg PA
CBHW020758230426
43666CB00007B/743